Y0-BVO-637

Azusa Street Mission

The Women
of Azusa Street

BR
1644
.A42
2005
west

Estrelda Alexander

The Pilgrim Press
Cleveland

To my husband Clem, without whose patience, love, and support this book would not have been possible.

The Pilgrim Press, 700 Prospect Avenue, Cleveland, Ohio 44115,

thepilgrimpress.com

© 2005 by Estrelda Alexander

Photographs on the cover: Top left to right: Jennie Evans Moore Seymour and Emma Cotton; bottom left to right: Rachel Harper Sizelove and Ardella Knapp Mead. Used by permission of the Flower Pentecostal Heritage Center.

All rights reserved. Published 2005

Printed in the United States of America on acid-free paper

10 09 08 07 06 05   5 4 3 2 1

Library of Congress Cataloging-in-Publication Data

Alexander, Estrelda, 1949–
    The women of Azusa Street / Estrelda Alexander.
       p. cm.
    ISBN 0-8298-1685-2 (alk. paper)
    1. Pentecostal women—United States—History—20th century.
    2. Pentecostalism—United States—History—20th century.   I. Title.
BR1644.A42 2005
289.9'4'0820973—dc22   2005022008

Contents

List of Illustrations

Introduction

THE AZUSA STREET REVIVAL began in 1906 in Los Angeles, California, under the leadership of William Joseph Seymour and continued day and night for at least three years. It was characterized by the ecstatic worship, glossolalia (speaking in tongues), and instances of divine healing that have come to be the hallmark of popular notions of Pentecostalism. The revival was the culmination of a series of events that began to unfold a half-decade earlier, when on January 1, 1901, students at Charles Fox Parham's healing home and Bible school experienced an outbreak of tongues speaking, which was identified as the "initial evidence" of Holy Spirit baptism. Though the embers of the original episode seemed only to smolder for several years, the "fire on Azusa Street" subsequently broke out with such force that one hundred years later, Pentecostalism and its sister Charismatic and Neo-Pentecostal movements have become major forces in global Christianity.

Reflecting on this main beginning point of the modern Pentecostal movement, names and exploits of several prominent men come to mind. Charles Fox Parham, William Joseph Seymour, William Durham, Frank Bartleman, and J. B. Cashwell all are well-known for their roles. These men, along with others such as Charles Harrison Mason, Ambrose J. Tomlinson, Howard Goss, Garfield T. Haywood, Alfred Garr, and Frank Ewart, are renowned for their individual accomplishments and collective leadership. They helped move what began as a local-ized, relatively insignificant revival among "disinherited" wash-erwomen and maids to a worldwide movement that now touch-es the lives of nearly 500 million people—by some estimates, between one-fourth and one-third of the Christian world.

In the historiography regarding the Azusa Street Revival and early Pentecostalism, the women who played equally vital roles in every aspect of the unfolding of the fledgling movement have not been given the same recognition. These women, whose names remain largely unknown, were just as instrumental as the men in initiating the revival, bringing it to fruition, and ensuring that its message found its way around the country and the world. Yet, until now, their stories remained untold.

This volume is only the beginning of an attempt of a correc-tive. It seeks simply to unearth vital information that gives face and voice to a few of the women whose testimonies were buried with them. It is not in any way exhaustive, for there are many more stories to be told and many more facets to be explored regarding the lives of the women presented here.

Part One explores the role of two women in bringing the revival to pass. This role began to unfold several months before the meetings got underway. A woman was the catalyst for the move of William Joseph Seymour's ministry to Los Angeles. Neely Terry was a Los Angeles resident who belonged to a small Holiness church. While visiting with family in Houston, she met Seymour, who was standing in as interim pastor. On returning to Los Angeles, Terry convinced her pastor and congregation to invite Seymour to serve as associate pastor. Though he preached only one sermon in that church before being locked out, it was this invitation that brought Seymour to that city. Since Terry was a cousin to the Asberry family in whose home Seymour conduct-ed his initial Bible studies, she may have been instrumental in his finding a place to carry out his ministry after he was rejected by the congregation. It is not known, however, what role, if any, Terry actually played in the revival.

The church where Seymour was first invited to speak in Los Angeles was pastored by a woman, Julia Hutchins. Though Hutchins and the congregation initially rejected Seymour's message of initial evidence, sometime after the revival started Hutchins was converted to the Pentecostal understanding of Holy Spirit baptism. She became a regular participant in the Azusa Street Revival and a solid supporter of Seymour's ministry. She was instrumental in taking the Pentecostal message from Azusa Street to Africa.

In Part Two, "At the Revival," we look at two women—Lucy Farrow and Clara Lum—who made major contributions to the success of the ongoing meetings and the Azusa Street church that was its home base. Lucy Farrow had been the pastor of William Seymour's church in Houston before he began attending Parham's Bible school in 1905. It was Farrow who introduced Seymour to the doctrine and experience of the baptism of the Holy Spirit with tongues as initial evidence. Subsequently, she introduced Seymour to Parham, thus setting up the chain of events that ultimately led to the beginning of the Azusa Street meeting. Farrow re-associated with Seymour at Azusa Street when he contacted Parham for help with his, at first, floundering meeting, and Parham responded by pairing Farrow with fellow evangelist J. A. Warren, Jr., and sending them to Seymour's aid. From that point on, the revival took off. Besides serving on the governing board of the mission and assisting in the worship services, Clara Lum served as its secretary and co-editor of the church newsletter, *The Apostolic Faith,* from 1906–8.

Within the revival, white women from various walks of life ministered alongside black washerwomen and household servants with no formal Bible or theological training. Both were given free reign to exercise their ministry gifts of speaking in tongues, interpreting glossolalic messages, prophesy, and intercession. They could also be found at the altar praying with new converts and seekers for the baptism of the Holy Spirit and healing. In fact, one element of the revival that drew public attention

—and a degree of derision of the secular press—was the regular sight of white men, many of them somewhat prominent members of the clergy or community, kneeling before black women who prayed with them to receive prayer for Holy Spirit baptism.

Several of these women did not come to Azusa Street as novices but instead had experience in ministry as pastors and evangelists throughout the country. Four women—Anna Hall, Mabel Smith, Lucy Farrow, and Neely Terry—had been acquainted with Charles Parham's ministry in Houston, Texas, where they had already had the experience of speaking in tongues.

A number of them used their ministry gifts to preach, teach, and lead the congregation in worship and handle the administrative responsibilities for the mission church that housed it. Initially, six of the twelve elders at the Azusa Street Mission charged with examining potential missionaries and evangelists for ordination and other spiritual and administrative oversight were women. They included Jennie Evans Moore, May Evans, Phoebe Sergeant, Ophelia Wiley, Clara Lum, and Florence Crawford.

Further evidence of the inclusion of women in the leadership of the mission comes from an interesting sidelight. Disenchanted by the racial attitudes of some of the entrusted whites, Seymour later incorporated into the formal structure of the Azusa Street Mission governing documents directions that his successor should be a person of color. He did not specify a man of color, leaving room that possibly the person could be a woman. Perhaps the greatest evidence of Seymour's prophetic understanding of women's role in the revival and movement it helped birth is reflected in a statement in *The Apostolic Faith*:

Before Jesus ascended to heaven, holy anointing oil had never been poured on a woman's head; but before He organized His church. He called them all into the upper room, both men and women, and anointed them with the oil of the Holy Ghost, thus qualifying them all to minister in this Gospel. On the day of Pentecost they all preached through the power of the Holy Ghost. In Christ Jesus there is neither male nor female, all are one.[1]

Part Three looks at the move "From Azusa to the World." Several outstanding women were among the many evangelists and missionaries who went out from the Azusa Street Revival to take the message of Pentecostalism across the country and to every corner of the globe. Large numbers of women preachers went out to preach what they claimed to be the "full gospel"— their new Pentecostal experience. Some went as single missionaries or evangelists. These included Ivy Campbell, who preached in Ohio; Mabel Smith, who "preached nightly to overflowing crowds" in Chicago; Rachel Sizelove in Missouri, and Lucy Leatherman. Others, including Daisy Batman, May Evans, Ardella Meade, Lillian Garr, and Rosa de Lopez, went as part of husband and wife teams. Still others, like Farrow and Julia Hutchins, went as part of larger missionary endeavors.

Florence Crawford received the baptism of the Holy Spirit at the revival. At the same time, she reportedly was instantaneously healed from a variety of ailments. Some credit her with being the first of the Azusa Street converts to take the Pentecostal message on the revival circuit. Crawford was instrumental in distributing the monthly newspaper that chronicled the events of the revival to Seymour's supporters. Eventually she and Seymour had a breach in their relationship and Crawford left the Azusa Street Mission and Los Angeles and moved to Portland, where she set up her own ministry, which she named the Apostolic Faith Church.

Ophelia Wiley, a black preacher, singer, and songwriter, preached from time to time in the Azusa Street meetings and wrote articles for the newspaper, *The Apostolic Faith*. She also served as part of evangelistic teams to spread the news of the revival in various cities throughout the northwestern United States.

Ivy Campbell preached revivals throughout Ohio and Pennsylvania and won many to the Pentecostal experience. Regularly, pastors and other ministers received their experience of speaking in tongues in her meetings, and her ministry caused such a stir in Akron, Ohio, that the ministers in that city passed a resolution denouncing her.

Lucy Leatherman went to Jerusalem to minister to the Arab population. She also traveled with Brother and Sister Lopez to hold meetings in Greenwich, Connecticut, where the group met with considerable opposition, including charges of witchcraft and hypnotism.

Prominent among the couples who went out from Azusa Street were Samuel and Ardella Mead. These two were well-known pioneer Methodist missionaries to Africa before attending the Azusa Street Revival. They both received the Holy Spirit baptism there and stayed at the revival for some time, documenting what they heard from several tongues speakers as African dialects.

A. G. Garr and his wife Lillian went to Danville, Virginia, and then on to India, five weeks after receiving their Holy Spirit baptism. From India they went on to China where their meetings drew great crowds.

G. W. and Daisy Batman traveled with their three children to Liberia with Julia Hutchins and Lucy Farrow. The Batmans' story was reported in an issue of *The Apostolic Faith* as an example of how these couples were viewed as a ministry team, not simply as a minister and his wife.

G. W. and May Evans both served as part of the credentialing committee. May was the first white person to receive the baptism of the Holy Spirit under Seymour's ministry.

Some stayed closer to home. Anna Hall remained in Los Angeles ministering to Russian and French Arcadian congregations "in their own languages." Abundio Lopez and his wife Rosa preached in street meetings to reach the Latino population that had begun to come to the city. In the years surrounding the revival, Susie Valdez concentrated her ministry just east of Los Angeles in communities such as Riverside and San Bernardino. However, often traveling and working with her son, her ministry would eventually cover a much broader geographical sphere.

Part Four covers the waning years of the Azusa Street Mission—between 1910 and 1922—when Jennie Seymour served at its helm with her husband William.

After leaving the revival, Rachel Sizelove and her family returned to settle in Springfield, Missouri, the future headquarters of the Assemblies of God. Its location is considered by denominational leaders as the response of her prophetic vision of "a beautiful bubbling, sparkling fountain" in the heart of the city. According to her, it "spr[ung] up gradually, but irresistibly, and began to flow toward the East and toward the West, toward the North and toward the South until the whole land was deluged with living water."[2]

Jennie Evans Seymour died in 1936, three years after she relinquished leadership of the church. She served as pastor for eleven years. With her death, the legacy of women's leadership in the life and ministry of the Azusa Street Mission came to an end. That legacy has yet to be fully explored. It is important, however, that the task of such exploration be vigorously pursued as Pentecostal women are beginning to reclaim their place in the leadership of a movement that they were so vital in shaping. The women of Azusa Street were not bystanders or merely supporters. Their own words portray a level of commitment and involvement in every facet of ministry, despite restrictions that had found their way into the Pentecostal movement in its earliest stages.

To some degree, the reasons for the historical oversight are understandable. Outside of the information about them contained in correspondences filed to *The Apostolic Faith* and other newsletters, little tangible information has previously come to light. Primary sources focusing on the role of women had been limited, as is true throughout much of religious history.

One problem generally inherent in the process of researching evangelical religious movements is the lack of attention given to properly identifying women. Several names have been repeatedly misspelled in various secondary resources, making it difficult to sort out available data. In these same resources married women often do not stand as individuals but are identified only by initials or as "Mrs. So-and-So" in conjunction with their husband's name.[3] Addressing oversights such as these ties these women to the Azusa Street Mission and revival and highlights their contribution in taking the Pentecostal message from Azusa Street to the various arenas in which it found a home.

Even given these constraints, the work in no way explores the full legacy of the contribution of women to early Pentecostalism. It is important that such exploration be picked up and vigorously pursued as Pentecostal women are beginning to reclaim their place in the leadership of a movement that they were so vital in shaping. Unearthing and portraying the roles of the women who were in some way participants in the Azusa Street meetings is only a start in developing a more equitable picture of the roles they played in the development of one of the major religious movements of the last century.

PART ONE

Getting to Azusa Street

*A*mong many Pentecostal believers, the events that unfolded at a little converted livery stable on Azusa Street in a
rundown section of Los Angeles, California, were
undoubtedly providential. God's providence was assisted by
women and men who, in one way or another, were instrumental
in setting the stage for the revival. One of the key elements was
getting William Joseph Seymour from Houston to Los Angeles to
accept the position as pastor of a Holiness church. Otherwise,
one hundred years later, we might be talking about the great
Houston outpouring.

The Azusa Street Revival was the culmination of a series of
events that began with the nineteenth-century Holiness
Movement and ran through Charles Fox Parham's Topeka Bible
school revival and a number of smaller meetings held throughout
the Midwest. Parham's earlier efforts had initially met with little
success.

Through a series of events—which might on first glance
appear to be pure happenstance—two women proved to be crucial in navigating a scenario that placed Seymour in Los Angeles.
Seymour was poised to head the revival—a revival that would
change the face of American religion for the unforeseen future. If
Neely Terry and Julia Hutchins had done little else to fan the
fires of revivalism in Los Angeles, their agreement to invite
Seymour to the city was the pivotal event that set the revival in

full force. Parham had previously determined to retain Seymour in Houston to minister to blacks in that city. But Neely Terry's and Julia Hutchins' invitation, coupled with Parham's vision of gaining new territory for his then-flagging movement, was an opportunity that could not be turned down. The future for Parham's message and leadership appeared bright until Hutchins denounced it as out of line with her Holiness understandings. When Hutchins first washed her hands of Seymour, Terry used her connections to situate his prayer meeting at the Bonnie Brea Street house, which was to be the first home of the revival.

Eventually, Terry disappeared from the scene, and Hutchins would be won over to Seymour's camp. She became a staunch supporter and an avid participant in the revival services. Her newly found zeal caused her to join the steady stream of those who ventured forth as missionaries taking the message of Pentecostal Spirit baptism to Africa.

chapter 1

Neely Terry

NEELY TERRY WAS A MUSICIAN, but otherwise she played no major role in the revival worship services. She was not one of the six women on the early administrative board, and no material or historian names her as a leader at either the Bonnie Brae prayer meeting or the Azusa Street Mission. Neither is she identified as being an individual or part of one of the evangelistic or missions teams that went out from the revival to spread its fires. She was not a pastor, an evangelist, or even a preacher. We have no recorded testimony from Terry, nor did she file any report back to *The Apostolic Faith* about any ministry in which she was engaged outside the mission. Besides this, there are no known extant photographs of her.

This elusive figure in early Pentecostal historiography generally receives only a footnote, or at most a paragraph, in most material on the revival. On first consideration, it might seem, therefore, that her role in shaping the Azusa Street Revival was inconsequential. Yet, her importance in the unfolding of events in Los Angeles and the life and ministry of William Seymour should not be underestimated. Terry was key in getting Seymour to Los Angeles and providing a place for his ministry to take root. For Terry links Seymour with three people—Julia Hutchins and Richard and Ruth Asberry—who were, themselves, significant in the ministry of Seymour and the development of events leading up to and fueling the Azusa Street Revival.

Terry was a resident of Los Angeles and part of the band of no more than twenty-five individuals who made up Julia Hutchins' Holiness congregation. Like the others, she and her family had been members of the Baptist church where Hutchins began to promote the doctrine of sanctification. Her family was one of the eight families that had been asked to leave the congregation when they accepted Hutchins' Holiness beliefs. Though the group was black, they worshiped for a short time at William Manley's predominantly white Household of Faith Mission. Subsequently, when the racial climate there became uncomfortable, her family was among those who helped Hutchins organize a black Church of the Nazarene congregation.

In the summer of 1905, soon after the congregation was organized, Terry left Los Angeles to visit family in Houston. While there, she reportedly worked as a cook for the Charles Fox Parham family.[1] It was possibly through their shared status as Parham's employees that Terry met Lucy Farrow, who may have invited Terry to attend worship services at the Holiness church, where she pastored.

Terry may have made the little Holiness congregation pastored by Lucy Farrow her spiritual home base while in Houston, or at least she worshiped there several times. On at least one visit, Terry encountered William Seymour. Farrow had left Houston for a while to accompany the Parham family to Kansas as their governess. In her absence, she turned her pulpit over to the care of Seymour. On this Sunday, he was the preacher.

Sometime during this period, however, Terry had her own Pentecostal Spirit baptism in tongues and spoke either while still visiting the Farrow congregation when Farrow returned and testified of her encounter, or in Parham's evening evangelistic services.

Terry returned home to Los Angeles in winter of 1906 after an extended stay in Houston. She was excited about her renewed spiritual encounter and enthusiastically told the small congregation about the experience she had had with speaking in tongues in Houston. Her enthusiasm was somewhat daunted, however, when she found her home congregation facing a season of spiritual discontent and frustration. Hutchins was having trouble leading the congregation and felt that she needed some help. When Hutchins suggested that the congregation might need a male minister who was strong in faith to come and assist with the new work, Terry remembered Seymour from her time in Houston and eagerly suggested his name.

Quite possibly, at the time Terry heard Seymour preach, he had not yet adopted this new understanding of initial evidence since he had not yet spoken in tongues himself. Or, perhaps as Alex Bills suggests, having received her own Pentecostal experience, either under the ministry of Farrow or Parham, Terry did not fully understand the important distinction between the Holiness understanding of Holy Spirit baptism tied to an inner witness of sanctification, which was her earlier experience, and the implications of Seymour and Parham's understanding of tongues, which her later experience included, so failed to mention this to Hutchins.[2] She probably simply considered tongues a deeper expression of the ecstatic expression that characterized much of black Holiness worship at that time.

In any case, evidently Hutchins trusted Terry's assessment of Seymour as a man of integrity and an anointed preacher. After a short period of prayer and consideration, and on Terry's recommendation, Hutchins and the congregation invited Seymour to Los Angeles. So after a short time in Parham's Houston Bible Training School, Brother Seymour received a letter from Mrs. Terry asking him to consider coming to California to help with the work.

Since Seymour did not have enough money to make the trip, he turned to Parham, his newly found spiritual mentor, for assistance. Parham provided him with one-way train fare, and Seymour began the trip. This was to be the first crucial connection for Seymour, who later was to reflect on this invitation as being providential. For as he saw it, "It was the divine call that brought me from Houston to Los Angeles. The Lord put it on the heart of one of the saints in Los Angeles to write to me that she felt the Lord wanted me to come there, and I felt that was the leading of the Lord. The Lord provided me the means and I came to take charge of a mission on Santa Fe Street."[3]

Seymour's welcome by Hutchins' congregation was short-lived, for the distinction of understandings between Holy Spirit baptism being simply an inner witness and it involving the initial evidence of speaking in tongues was important to Hutchins and some members of her congregation. On the first Sunday morning, Seymour preached from the second chapter of Acts with an emphasis on speaking in tongues as initial evidence of Holy Spirit baptism. This message placed him at odds with Pastor Hutchins, who denied him further access to the pulpit of the little congregation. Whatever arrangements had been made for lodging were also cancelled.

Not everyone in the congregation was put off by his preaching. Yet once Seymour was locked out of Hutchins' church, he found himself with few allies in the city (except Terry), no train fare back to Houston, and no place either to preach or stay. Terry probably felt both some loyalty and a sense of obligation to him since it was her suggestion that brought him to the city in the first place.

Perhaps with only a little influence from Terry, one member of Hutchins' group, Brother Lee, acted out of Christian charity to solve at least one of Seymour's problems. Though he was not entirely convinced of the truthfulness of Seymour's doctrine, he offered him a place to stay until he could find accommodations elsewhere.

With Seymour having his own physical need for shelter met, temporarily at least, Terry could turn her attention to making a second crucial connection and securing a place for Seymour's ministry. She probably influenced her cousin, Ruth Asberry, along with her husband Richard to provide this opportunity. The Asberrys had also been members of the Baptist congregation and subsequently of Hutchins' group. Since the Asberrys had only heard Seymour speak on that one occasion and had had little time to get acquainted with him, Terry may have persuaded them to invite him to hold his meeting at their home. In early April, the couple opened their home on Bonnie Brae Street for Seymour to hold a Bible study. This invitation set the stage for the outbreak of revival. For it was here that the band of mostly female African American household workers began to gather and seek God for a new experience of the Spirit. Though Terry reportedly received the experience in Houston, she was probably among this group.

Seymour's association with Lee proved to be providential for the group of Seymour followers. For the Lee home was located just down the block for the prayer-meeting site. And it was Lee who was the first of the group to receive the Pentecostal experience of tongues in his own home when either Seymour or Farrow, or both, laid hands on him to receive the baptism of the Holy Spirit. He immediately ran down the street to share his experience with those who had gathered for prayer at the Asberry home. This was just the catalyst they needed to ignite the fire of revival!

One by one, as people began to experience speaking in tongues, the small group grew—first filling the double parlor of the house, then ultimately overflowing into the outdoors. When the prayer meeting spilled out onto the porch, the street in front of the house was filled with seekers and onlookers drawn by the strange sights and sounds of the meeting. Within a few days the meeting was too full to be contained at the home location, and new quarters had to be found. It is here that we lose contact with Terry, and her name does not surface again in any of the reports concerning the revival. Yet even with the little we know of her, one wonders how the revival would have unfolded had she not made these important links.

chapter 2

Julia Hutchins

JULIA HUTCHINS' PARTICIPATION in the Azusa Street Revival and its evangelistic afterthrust is an ironic turn of events that the saints would say could only be ordered and ordained by God and might not have happened except for a sudden change of heart on her part. For a variety of reasons, however, most Azusa Street historians pay little attention to Julia Hutchins' role at the Azusa Street meetings. They see her primarily as the woman pastor whose little Holiness congregation was instrumental in issuing the invitation that initially brought Seymour to Los Angeles. Yet, they quickly note that she soon disassociated herself from Seymour over his teaching about the initial evidence of tongues for the baptism of the Holy Spirit. What many of these same historians fail to report is that Hutchins later reconciled with Seymour, received the Pentecostal experience of tongues, spent time at the Azusa Street meetings, and went out from there as part of the vast army that carried the message of the revival around the world.

Like several of the other women, little is known of Hutchins' personal life during the time of the revival. We know that she was married to a man who at one time was considered a backslider, but he was probably restored to Christian faith during the revival. But we don't even have his name. Furthermore, little is known of her actual role in the revival itself. It is known, however, that by her own testimony, Hutchins was saved in July

1901. At the same time she felt called to go to Africa. Two years later, in July 1903, she experienced sanctification and a renewal of her call to Africa.

The involvement of Julia Hutchins in the Azusa Street Revival might never have happened were it not for a change of heart that she experienced somewhere between her first encounter with William Seymour and the start of the revival. After Hutchins' initial opposition to Seymour's teaching on initial evidence faded, she proved to be very instrumental in its spread throughout the Holiness community of Los Angeles. Among the people affiliated with Hutchins, several were to play roles in the unfolding of the Azusa Street Revival. The number of people from her mission that showed up in Seymour's congregation indicates that she probably folded her church and blended it into Seymour's, at least for a short duration.

She also personally introduced Seymour to some prominent holiness leaders in the city. Though, like Hutchins, their initial reaction to Seymour's teaching was skeptical, the very exposure was pivotal in providing an audience for his teaching throughout the Los Angeles Holiness community. Neely Terry was the catalyst for Hutchins' invitation to Seymour to come to Los Angeles. Ruth and Richard Asberry allowed him to use their house at 214 Bonnie Brae Street to hold his nightly Bible study that witnessed the outbreak of occurrences of tongues speaking that was the catalyst for the Azusa Street Revival.

Hutchins' early understanding of Holy Spirit baptism differed markedly from Seymour's in one essential element: the necessity for the initial evidence of speaking in tongues to demonstrate that one had been filled. Hutchins, like many other Holiness proponents of her day, believed strongly that one needed the baptism of the Holy Spirit. But she, and they, believed that the proof of such baptism was an inner witness and a piety of life rather than any outward visible manifestation. Hutchins and several of the members of her congregation felt that they had already received the baptism of the Holy Spirit when they had been sanctified. So when Seymour came preaching that the baptism of the Holy Spirit should be accompanied by glossolalia, Hutchins and her congregation were disturbed by what they understood as an inference that they had not yet been baptized in the Holy Spirit.

Hutchins came to the pastorate of her congregation through a series of schisms. At first she had been completely on the outside of an earlier theological disagreement over tenets of the Holiness faith. Prior to 1905, she had been a member of Second Baptist Church in Los Angeles. This congregation was the first African American Baptist church and the second black congregation in that city. Hutchins was a respected member of the congregation and an itinerant evangelist who presumably upheld a baptistic understanding of salvation and Christian piety. But in that year she was converted to and began teaching the doctrine of sanctification as a second work of grace.

This deviation from traditional Baptist doctrine did not stand her in good stead with her pastor, C. H. Anderson, or with several other members of the congregation. She was counseled to desist from teaching the new understanding, but when she would not, Hutchins and eight other families whose members sympathized with her, were removed of their fellowship.

Like Hutchins, these disenfranchised members were African American. Yet, for a time, they chose to associate with and worship at the Household of Faith Mission, a predominantly white congregation pastored by William Manley. Though the racial climate of Los Angeles was much more open than in many other parts of the country, and race relations within the Holiness movement were considerably more cordial than in other denominations, the mission was not completely free of discrimination. Regardless of calling or gifting, blacks were still generally relegated to secondary roles and subjected to slight indignities because of personal prejudices of some members. Their group soon separated and began to worship in a tent in a black neighborhood in downtown Los Angeles. They appointed Hutchins as their pastor.

Seymour's Bible study at Richard and Ruth Asberry's home was not the first such meeting at that address. During the winter of 1905, even in warm southern California, the tent that served as the home for Hutchins' little congregation proved to be no match for the chilled night weather. The Asberrys were members of the upstart congregation and offered their home as a temporary base for its ministry. It was here that an event occurred that was to have a far-reaching effect on the ministry of the Azusa Street Mission. On Monday nights the group regularly held evangelistic services in an attempt to reach people in the community. The first portion of these meetings consisted of a song service held on the front porch. The exuberant singers were effective in regularly drawing the attention of neighbors, who would gather in the street and on their porches to listen. They would then be invited into the house for the remainder of the service, which consisted of preaching and prayer. The group's evangelistic efforts proved so successful that after a short time the group had outgrown the house-meeting facilities and looked for larger space. They found it at Ninth and Santa Fe Street, and Hutchins leased the facility. This is the location where Seymour came to preach.

Among those won to Christ through the efforts of this little group was Jennie Evans Moore, who resided across the street at 217 Bonnie Brae. Moore was to later become Seymour's wife and play a pivotal role in the ministry and leadership of the mission.

For a time, Moore was a member of Hutchins' congregation, but shortly she started attending Joseph Smale's church. She may have found herself among a group of Hutchins followers who began to express a degree of dissatisfaction in early 1906. The group's discontent left Hutchins feeling a need for a strong male to help lead the body. She began to look around for someone to assist her.

Seemingly without awareness of the important distinction between the doctrine of initial evidence of tongues with Holy

Spirit baptism and the Holiness understanding of an inner witness of sanctification, Neely Terry, a member of Hutchins'
group, suggested that the congregation invite Seymour to Los
Angeles to serve as an associate pastor. After a short period of
prayerful consideration, Hutchins issued the invitation on behalf
of the congregation but could not afford to offer Seymour the
financial resources for making the trip from Houston. So
Seymour had to get train fare from Charles Parham, his teacher
and mentor.

Once in Los Angeles, Seymour came to the church on Sunday
morning to preach his first sermon. His text was from Joel 2:28,
and he clearly implied that speaking in tongues was the initial
evidence of Holy Spirit baptism. Hutchins' congregation was
appalled at the implication that they had not received God's
fullest provision. When Seymour returned that evening to preach
a second sermon, he found that the doors were locked and he
would no longer be allowed to address the congregation.

Without attempting to promote Seymour's theology,
Hutchins took a step that gave him an even larger audience for
his message. In an attempt to settle the validity of his claims
once and for all, Hutchins arranged a meeting between Seymour
and local Holiness leaders two months before his meeting
moved to Azusa Street. T. M. Roberts, president of the Southern
California Holiness Association, was not convinced by
Seymour's position and forbade him to continue teaching it
within the Holiness movement. Seymour complied with the
request and did not attempt to contact other Holiness congregations, but exposure in this meeting gave vent to his ideas among
a number of Holiness preachers. Since not all the leaders dismissed his contention out of hand, their very exposure to his
ideas assured that news of the new teaching would make the
rounds. Because of this, several would later come to his meetings, not as seekers but as skeptical observers. Others came, at
first drawn by the sheer strangeness of the tongues phenomenon. Some among these two groups accepted Seymour's theolo-

gy and received the Pentecostal experience. A few remained at the mission as supporters.

For the moment, however, Seymour was left without a base for ministry in the city. Very shortly, though, Seymour found refuge for both his body and ministry in two homes that were residences of members of Hutchins' church. Edward Lee and his wife invited Seymour to stay in their home, providing him with the essential physical shelter that his body required. The invitation of Richard and Ruth Asberry was to prove to be even more providential to the new Los Angeles arrival. It was here that Seymour began to teach the Bible study that exploded into the Azusa Street Revival.

It is not known whether Hutchins ever attended Seymour's meetings at Bonnie Brae Street. At some point between the time that Seymour was locked out of Hutchins' church and the Azusa Street Revival moved into full swing, Hutchins became a whole-hearted supporter of Seymour and a convert to his understanding of tongues as initial evidence. Following that change of mind and heart, she was a regular participant in the Azusa Street Revival, sought and received the experience herself, and took the Pentecostal message from Azusa Street to Africa.

It isn't known how long Hutchins stayed at Azusa Street or what role she played there. She was among those believed to have received the gift of xenolalia sometime during the revival. In an article in *The Apostolic Faith,* she was reported to have "received the gift of the Uganda language."[1]

Hutchins saw this language endowment as confirmation that God had called her to Africa when she was saved and affirmed that call at her sanctification. Armed with this gift and faith that God would provide for their needs, and accompanied by her husband and young niece, Leila McKinney, she left for Africa in September 1906. This trip gave her no occasion to prove the gift of xenolalia, for the country of Liberia to which Hutchins felt called and traveled had English for its official language.

On her way, she stopped and preached in several cities in the

United States, including Chattanooga, Tennessee, and New York. At each stop the group held a series of revival services. These services were considered a spiritual success because a number of people were converted, sanctified, and received the Holy Spirit baptism and tongues. They also functioned as a successful means of raising funds to support the "faith" journey that had no other visible means of support.

The Apostolic Faith newsletter reported on her venture in a short insert entitled "Testimonies of Outgoing Missionaries":

> A company of three missionaries left Los Angeles September 13, en route for the west coast of Africa. Sister Hutchins has been preaching the Gospel in the power of the Spirit. She has received the baptism with the Holy Ghost and the gift of the Uganda language, the language of the people to whom she is sent. A brother who has been in that country understands and has interpreted the language she speaks. Her husband is with her and her niece, who also has been given the African language.[2]

In New York, Hutchins' party joined up with another party from Azusa Street led by S. J. Mead and held a meeting that lasted two weeks. While in that city, Hutchins filed back the simple report about the earlier Chattanooga meeting:

> The Lord used us to His glory in Chattanooga. He set that town on fire. Praise His name. The dear ones did not want to see us leave, but the will of God must be done. The last meeting we had with the people was beside the train that brought us away. Under the shed there was where the Lord used me last in that city. He sang and preached through me and some confessed their sins and asked, what shall I do to be saved? Some promised to live a better life. O glory to Jesus. While on the train, we preached the Word and some received it with joy. We hope to set sail for Africa soon. Pray that God may use us on the boat to the salvation of souls. Love to all the dear saints.[3]

A participant in the Chattanooga meeting sent a letter to the editors of *The Apostolic Faith,* a portion of which concerned the meetings: "The Lord has been working in Chattanooga, Tenn., where a band of Africa missionaries stopped on their way. Souls have been saved, a number have been baptized with the Holy Ghost and received the Bible evidence."[4]

Leaving New York, the group proceeded together across the Atlantic by steamer, stopping in Liverpool, England. As was the pattern, the entire party stayed in Liverpool a short time waiting for passage to Africa. They spent that period holding services among the African immigrants. Then the party regrouped. The Hutchins family and Farrow went to Liberia, and the Meads proceeded to Angola with their party.

On the way to Africa, Hutchins kept a journal in which she wrote her testimony of her salvation, sanctification, and Holy Spirit baptism. She sent it back to the group at Azusa Street, where excerpts from it were published in *The Apostolic Faith* newsletter as "Sister Hutchins' Testimony":

I was justified on the 4th of July, 1901, and at that time, I felt that the Lord wanted me in Africa, but I was not then at all willing to go. But on the 28th of July, 1903, the Lord sanctified me. Before He sanctified me, He asked me if I would go to Africa. I promised Him I would. From that time on, I have felt the call to Africa, and have been willing to go at any moment, but not knowing just when the Lord would have me leave.

On the sixth of last month, while out in my back yard one afternoon, I heard a voice speaking to me these words: "On the 15th day of September, take your husband and baby and start out for Africa." And I looked around and about me to see if there was not someone speaking to me, but I did not see anyone, and I soon recognized that it was the voice of God. I looked up into the heavens and said: "Lord, I will obey." Since then I have had many tests and temptations from the devil. He has at times told me that I would not even live to see the 15th of September, but I never once doubted God. I knew that He was able to bring everything to pass that He told me to do.

After hearing the voice telling me to leave Los Angeles. . . , I went to one of my neighbors and testified to her that the Lord had told me to leave for Africa. . . . She looked at me with a smile. I asked her what she was smiling about. She said: "Because you have not got street car fare to go to Azusa Street Mission tonight, and talking about going to Africa." But I told her I was trusting in a God that could bring all things to pass that He wanted us to do. He has really supplied all my needs in every way, for the work where He has called me.

I want to testify also about my husband. He was a backslider, and how the devil did test me, saying: "You are going out to cast the devil out of others, and going to take a devil with you." My husband was not saved, but I held on to God and said: "Lord, I will obey."

I continued to testify and to make preparations to leave on the 15th. The Lord reclaimed my husband and sanctified him wholly and put the glory and shout in him. So now it is my time to laugh. The devil has oppressed and mocked me; but praise the Lord, now I can mock him. Glory to God!

It is now ten minutes to four o'clock in the afternoon on the 15th day of September. I am all ready and down to the Mission with my ticket and everything prepared, waiting to have hands laid on and the prayers of the saints, and expect to leave at eight o'clock from the Santa Fe station en route for Africa. We expect to go to Mt. Coffee, Monrovia, Liberia.

Feeling the need of a real companion in the Gospel that was out and out for God, I prayed to God that He might give me one to go with me. I had my eyes upon one that I wanted to go, but in prayer and humility before God, I found out it was not the one the Lord wanted to go. So I said: "Anyone, Lord, that you would have to go will be pleasing to me." And, to my surprise, He gave me my niece—a girl that I had raised from a child. Now she is nineteen years of age, is saved, sanctified and baptized with the

Holy Ghost, and is going with me out into the work of the Lord. So instead of giving me one companion, He gave me two—my niece and my husband.

. . . I want the prayers of the saints that I may stay humble.

Mrs. J. W. Hutchins.[5]

Leila McKinney, the niece named in the letter, accompanied Hutchins to Liberia. Her testimony, "A Girl's Consecration for Africa," appeared below her aunt's.

I am saved, sanctified and baptized with the Holy Ghost and have the Bible evidence. The Lord showed me that the language I spoke was the language of Africa. My aunt who has been the same as a mother to me, was going to Africa. I asked the Lord if He wanted me to go, to open up a way for me, and the next morning He opened the way for me. I did not have the means and He gave me the fare and supplied all my needs. I am willing to trust Him through to Africa. I know the Lord wants me to go there. I want to testify to those people and teach the children about the blessed Lord, and to work for the Lord. I am willing to forsake all my loved ones for His sake. I want the saints to pray for me for I am young in the Lord.

Leila McKinney.[6]

An article entitled "Speeding to Foreign Lands" in *The Apostolic Faith* featured a letter written by Hutchins just as her party was ready to leave England for Monrovia. It was dated December 16, 1906, and was sent from Liverpool.

I write to let you know something of the way the Lord has been dealing with us on the way.

We held a meeting in New York lasting almost two weeks and had the pleasure of seeing many sanctified and quite a number receive their Pentecost. One dear sister who had been seeking for a number of days began to sing and sang almost an hour and her husband spoke in a tongue which sounded like Hebrew. Another brother was hugging him and he began to speak in the tongues and they conversed in this tongue for a while.

A wealthy lady was sanctified and received her Pentecost in a short time, her servant was seeking, and just as her mistress jumped up, she too was on her feet and the two began to praise God together and speak in tongues. . . . The same night, a friend of this lady went to her home and during a night of prayer, she laid hands on the brother and he received his Pentecost and began to speak with tongues and glorify God.

When we went to the steamer, a large number of the saints gathered and we had quite a time saying good-bye to all the dear ones. We realized we were blest by meeting them. May God continue to use them in the future as He has in the past.

We arrived here yesterday morning safely and shall stay until the steamer sails for Africa next Saturday. We have held a service for natives of Africa. He careth for us faithfully day by day.

Yours in Christ,

Mrs. J.W. Hutchins[7]

The final correspondence from the group in Liberia appearing in *The Apostolic Faith* was an unsigned report simply titled "In Africa." It was dated March 26, six months after Hutchins began her trip, and was written from Monrovia.

[W]e opened a ten day meeting in a school house, and on the tenth night, the Lord came in mighty power. Two were baptized with the Holy Ghost and spoke in tongues. Ten here have received sanctification, and five are filled with the Holy Ghost and speaking in tongues. A brother and his household have been baptized with the Holy Ghost. God has called him to the ministry and he will be baptized Sunday the 30th of March. Have been holding meetings going on three months. The Lord is sending a crowd of the African natives to the meeting and He is working wonderfully with them. The house is filled with the natives every service and they are being saved and sanctified and filled with the Holy Ghost and healed of all manner of diseases. The Lord surely is working with the native Africans of this land. All the saints send love.[8]

By today's standards, Hutchins' missionary efforts apparently yielded only small fruit: a hundred or so saved, several dozen people sanctified, and several more receiving their Pentecostal experience. We do not know how long Julia Hutchins stayed in Liberia, for whether she returned with Lucy Farrow is not reported. Like so many of the women, we simply lose track of her.

PART TWO

At the Revival

ay and night, seven days a week, for more than seven years, they gathered in the renovated livery stable to take part in a move ordained by God and unparalleled in the American religious experience. They came from all over the country and the world to share in a never-to-be-repeated Holy Spirit outpouring reminiscent of the Upper Room on the Day of Pentecost.

Men and women, adults and children, black, white, yellow, and red freely worshiped God and admonished each other to holiness of life through speaking in tongues and interpretation, through prophetic pronouncements, through testimony, song, prayer, miraculous signs, and preaching. Each one, in order as directed by the Holy Spirit, gave vent to the fire that was shut deep within their bones and glorified God for their new found freedom and empowerment.

Though Seymour was pastor of the flock, many contend that "there was no leader, except the Holy Ghost." God used women as well as men, without distinction of class or social status in a dramatic demonstration of power. Black washerwomen prayed with white pastors of prominent congregations; young girls prophetically confronted seasoned men with messages that brought them to repentance and renewed spiritual vitality. Seasoned women preachers like Lucy Farrow, Julia Hutchins, Anna Hall, Ardella Mead, Mabel Smith, Lillian Garr, and Ivey

Campbell worked alongside newly empowered novices such as Jennie Moore and Florence Crawford. They were involved in every aspect of the work. Besides exhorting and preaching, they served on the administrative board, helped edit and publish the newspaper that heralded news of the revival to thousands of supporters, and maintained the mailing list that supported it. They gave and interpreted messages in tongues and tirelessly worked the altar to pray with seekers for salvation and Holy Spirit baptism.

At a time when the larger society was still wrestling with the issue of a woman's rightful place, these women found a place for themselves at Azusa Street. While most denominations had not begun to ordain women or allow them in the pulpit, these women claimed for themselves ordination by God and made a pulpit wherever they found themselves at the Azusa Street Mission and on the surrounding streets and campgrounds.

chapter 3

Lucy Farrow

ONE OF THE MOST RESPECTED WOMEN—or men—at Azusa Street was pastor and evangelist Lucy Farrow, who variably has been referred to as "the central prophet igniting the Holy Ghost fires in Southern California,"[1] the "first key networker and 'prayer warrior' of the Pentecostal movement,"[2] and the "first major personality in the black Pentecostal movement."[3] Farrow holds a very important yet often overlooked place in the beginning of the Pentecostal movement and in Seymour's life and ministry. For without her introducing him to the doctrine and experience of tongues as initial evidence and to its then chief proponent, Charles Fox Parham, Seymour might have remained an itinerant Holiness preacher assisting from time to time in her little Holiness mission in Texas.

Compared to most of the other African American women associated with Seymour and the Azusa Street Mission and Revival, we know a great deal about her work and ministry. Yet we know little about her as a person, especially the first twenty years of her life. We have no information about her early family life, spiritual experience, or educational attainment. Farrow was born in Norfolk, Virginia, in 1851, fifteen years before the end of the American Civil War. Reportedly, she was the niece of the famed abolitionist Frederick Douglass[4] and was either born as a slave or was later sold in slavery. One theory is that she was the daughter of a white slave owner and a slave woman; although she enjoyed freedom during her father's lifetime, she was sold into slavery after his death.[5]

In 1871, Farrow was living in Mississippi where her son James Pointer was born, so presumably she was married by that time. Eventually, she had migrated to Houston, Texas, and could be found there in 1890. By that time, she was widowed at least once and had borne seven children, though by then only two remained alive. In Houston Farrow lived with James and his wife Florence while she pastored a little Holiness mission church. The only written description of her refers to Farrow as a mulatto,[6] an indication that she was a fairly light-skinned black woman. The only available photograph of Farrow is a group portrait of the early Azusa Street Mission administrative board.

The difficulty of tracing Farrow's roots lies partly in the problem of correctly recording names in primary and secondary sources. For example, while Robert Owens gives Farrow's full name as April Lucy Farrow,[7] in most sources she is identified simply as Lucy Farrow. Emma Cotton, an eyewitness to the revival who recalls the event in writing thirty years later and gives Farrow a prominent place, refers to her as "Sis Farrah,"[8] and Lucy Leatherman identifies the woman who laid hands on her to receive the Holy Spirit baptism as "Sister Ferrell."[9]

Farrow was among the oldest of the Azusa Street leaders and was already fifty-six years old when she got to Los Angeles. She did not come to Azusa Street as a novice but instead as an experienced evangelist and pastor. She introduced Seymour to the Pentecostal understanding of Holy Spirit baptism while he was a member of her church in Houston. Seymour was more than just a bench member. He was a mature Christian who became a valuable part of the congregation, filling in for her when Farrow went to Kansas.

Farrow had met Charles Parham when he had come to Houston to conduct evangelistic services. When he left to go home to Kansas for a while, he needed someone to assist with family chores. Possibly because she needed the money, Farrow left her pulpit in Seymour's care to accompany the Parham family to Topeka to serve as governess and cook for the Bible school. In that capacity, she was able to regularly listen to Parham expound on his theological ideas, including his new understanding of tongues as initial evidence of Holy Spirit baptism. When Parham returned to Houston in 1905 to set up a second Bible school and hold a series of revival meetings in which he preached his two major doctrines of initial evidence and divine healing, Farrow returned with him. In the racially segregated climate in the early 1900s American South, the Bible school classes were attended only by whites, but the evening worship services had at least a small number of African Americans in attendance. It was in one of these services that Farrow had heard Parham speak and became convinced of the truth of his message. When she accompanied the Parhams to Topeka, she experienced the same pattern of racial segregation that she had found in Houston. But it was in one of these racially mixed meetings in nearby Baxter Springs that she had her Pentecostal experience, becoming the first recorded black person to have the experience.

After receiving the experience of speaking in tongues, Farrow returned to Houston, where she remained active for some time as a Holiness pastor. Farrow can be credited to a large degree from moving Seymour from the Holiness to the Pentecostal camp. Prior to meeting her, Seymour most likely held the Holiness understanding that sanctification and Holy Spirit baptism were the same experience, and that evidence of the experience was an inner witness of the Spirit and a life lived in submission to God's will. Farrow shared her testimony with Seymour and the others in her congregation, convincing them that tongues were a necessary and authentic expression of Holy Spirit baptism.[10] Seymour also heard her speak in tongues in worship services of the little mission. When he questioned Farrow about the experience, she explained what she had learned from Parham about the doctrine of initial evidence. She later introduced the two men to each other and was instrumental in getting Seymour enrolled in the school.[11] This meeting set up the chain of events that ultimately led to the beginning of the Azusa Street meeting.

While Farrow was away, Neely Terry visited Farrow's church and heard Seymour preach. Several months later she would recommend that Seymour be invited to Los Angeles. Terry returned to Los Angeles to find her home church in turmoil and in need of assistance from a seasoned minister. Terry convinced her pastor, Julia Hutchins, and the congregation to invite Seymour to come help them.

The timing of Farrow's arrival in Los Angeles is disputed. Some scholars indicate that she arrived after Seymour's group had moved to Azusa Street.[12] Most eyewitness accounts, however, place her at the earlier Bonnie Brae meeting. According to them, once Seymour arrived in Los Angeles, and after he had been ousted by Pastor Hutchins, he initially experienced only limited success in his quickly convened prayer meetings. In this scenario, while Seymour's group was still meeting in the Bonnie Brae Street home, and after several days of seeking the experience of speaking in tongues, no one had received it. A somewhat frustrated Seymour wired to Parham in Houston to send help for the work. Farrow was dispatched along with Joseph Warren, a close friend of Seymour.

Seymour must have been excited to see his former pastor and mentor. He knew she would add greatly to the ministry because, having already received the baptism of the Holy Spirit, Farrow was known for having the gift of impartation—laying on of hands for others to receive the experience. Her stirring testimonies of her own Holy Spirit baptism added fire to the fever pitch that the meetings had already reached. Within a few days of her arrival, the revival broke out in earnest and one person after another began receiving the Pentecostal experience of tongues. She stayed on to work beside Seymour as a preacher and teacher at the Azusa Street Meeting and became a central figure in the outpouring of the Holy Spirit. One source referred to her as "God's anointed handmaid, who came . . . from Houston

. . . bringing the full Gospel, and whom God has greatly used as she laid her hands on many who have received the Pentecost and the gift of tongues."[13]

Reportedly, one of those on whom she laid hands was Brother Lee, and Farrow's ministry to him is an example of her valuable role in the revival. Lee was the first person in Seymour's Bonnie Brae Street meeting—and therefore in Los Angeles—to speak in tongues in response to seeking this experience as an evidence of Holy Spirit baptism. According to some scholars and at least one eyewitness report, it was Farrow, not Seymour, who ministered this experience to him. Farrow was a guest in the Lee home, where Seymour had been staying. Seymour had previously laid hands on him and prayed for Holy Spirit baptism, and though he had a powerful spiritual experience, he did not speak in tongues at that time. One evening at his request, Farrow laid hands on Lee and he began speaking in tongues exuberantly. The event made such an impression on Emma Cotton that she recalls it thirty years later in her memoir. According to Cotton, Farrow and Seymour were eating dinner at the Lee home when, "Sister Farr[ow] rose from her seat, walked over to Brother Lee and said, 'The Lord tells me to lay hands on you for the Holy Ghost.' And when she laid hands on him, he fell out of his chair as though dead, and began to speak in other tongues."[14]

Lee left immediately for the Bonnie Brae Street prayer meeting at the Asberry home. When he arrived, he walked through the door with his hands raised, speaking in tongues. Cotton also reports that "the power fell on the others [who were gathered there], and all six people began to speak in tongues."[15] This experience was just the match needed to ignite an already simmering revival.

Farrow was only one of a number of women at Azusa Street who used their ministry gifts to preach, teach, and lead the congregation in worship and handle the administrative responsibilities for the mission church that housed it. All of them—black and white—were powerful examples of strong, spiritual women. But Farrow stood out for her spiritual leadership, especially among the black women, and was sought out by several people—black and white—who were themselves later to become prominent leaders in the Pentecostal movement. Accordingly, she received more extensive coverage (though much of it is cursory) in Pentecostal history than most of the other women associated with the Azusa Street Revival.

Within a few months of coming to Azusa Street, Farrow felt called to embark on a preaching campaign that included stops in Texas, Louisiana, North Carolina, Virginia, New York, and England on her way to Liberia. In Texas, in August 1906, she again rejoined Parham to work as part of the ministry team for one of his revivals. It was here that Howard Goss, an early Pentecostal leader who was a key figure in the expansion of the movement into the Midwest and one of the founders of the Assemblies of God, encountered Farrow.

According to Goss, in one of these meetings, Farrow once prayed for twenty-five people, all of whom received the gift of tongues. Goss had previously rejected the idea of initial evidence but progressively accepted Pentecostal doctrines. Farrow's sermon at Azusa Street convinced him of the truth of the doctrine and, according to his diary, as he witnessed fellow mourners lining up, being touched, and speaking in tongues, his "heart became hungry again for another manifestation of God. . . . So I went forward that she might place her hands upon me. When she did, the Spirit of God again struck me like a bolt of lightning; the Power of God surged through my body, and I again began speaking in tongues."[16]

Goss' wife Ethel, who encountered Farrow in the same meeting, reported that, "Although colored [sic], she was received as a messenger of the Lord to us, even in the [d]eep south of Texas."[17] While in Virginia, she stopped in Norfolk and nearby Portsmouth, holding successful revival services in which hundreds were saved and baptized with the Holy Spirit. By the time she left that state, two new congregations had been planted in those cities.[18]

In an article in *The Apostolic Faith* entitled "The Work in Virginia," Farrow uses her own words to detail the work in the tidewater area of the state. The short letter from Farrow was written from Portsmouth and was published in the October 1906 issue of the newsletter:

> We had a glorious meeting last night. It was the sixth night and we have six speaking in tongues. It is wonderful to see how the Lord is working with His believing children, but there is much to be done here. There is a band of saints that do not read the Bible like saints. They say the Bible is for unbelievers so they do not read it at all. O for some one to help. Won't you come and help if you can, and as soon as you can?
>
> God is making a short work in the earth today. He is soon coming to earth again. He said we should not get over the cities until the Son of Man should come, so we have not much time to lose. Remember me to all of the saints. Tell them to pray for me much. I can't write to all, so you remember me to all as one. Ask them to pray for the work in Virginia. It is much needed. I don't know how long the Lord is going to keep me here. There is so much to be done.
>
> I did not come through Danville, but I am going there as soon as I can get off from this place. I came through New Orleans and changed cars there, and laid hands on two sick, and sowed seed on the way from Houston here.
>
> Lucy Farrow.[19]

The success of Farrow's efforts in Virginia was attested to by a follow-up report that she filed back to the mission just before she embarked from New York to Africa. While the actual words of that report are not available, a summary in the December 1906 issue of *The Apostolic Faith* provides a glance at its contents: "Sister Lucy Farrow wrote from New York that she had started for Africa. About two hundred souls had been saved in Portsmouth and most of them were speaking in tongues. She sends love to the saints and asks your prayers."[20]

On arriving in Africa, Farrow stayed in Johnsonville, Liberia, twenty-five miles away from the capitol of Monrovia for seven months, working with Julia Hutchins and her husband and niece. Reportedly, during her tenure there, she experienced the xenolalic gift of the Kru language and was able to preach at least two messages to the Kru people in their own dialect. Also, reportedly, some of the Kru people to whom she ministered received the English language with their Holy Spirit baptism. During the revival in Liberia, it was reported that "twenty souls received their Pentecost [and] numbers were saved, sanctified and healed."[21]

After leaving Liberia, Farrow returned to Los Angeles by way of Virginia, North Carolina, and other areas of the South. In November 1907 she conducted a revival in Littleton, North Carolina. By May 1908, she had established a ministry that was closely linked to the Azusa Street Mission. She ministered from a "small faith cottage" located in back of the mission where people came to her for prayer, healing, and to receive the baptism of the Holy Spirit. As detailed in the final issue of *The Apostolic Faith* produced in Los Angeles:

> The Lord had baptized a number in the little faith cottage back of the Mission. He has used our dear Sister Farrow whom He sent from Texas at the beginning of the outpouring of the Spirit in Los Angeles. In her room in the cottage, quite a number have received a greater filling of the Spirit and some have been healed and baptized with the Spirit since she returned from Africa.[22]

Farrow returned to Houston and lived with her son and his wife. In 1911, only five years after the beginning of the Azusa Street Revival, she contracted intestinal tuberculosis. She died in February of that year at the age of sixty.

chapter 4

Clara Lum

AMONG THE WOMEN WHO WERE INVOLVED with the Azusa Street Revival, none was more valuable in keeping the news of its growth and spread before its anxiously awaiting supporters than Clara E. Lum, an itinerant evangelist who had been involved with several other prominent Holiness groups before finding her way to Azusa Street. Lum was born in Wisconsin in 1869. Her family moved to Oregon while Clara was a child. As a young woman, Lum was plagued by chronic health problems and moved to Los Angeles in the 1890s because of them. We do not know about her early religious affiliation or much about her educational attainment, though it is evident that Lum had achieved some level of early training, since shortly after coming to Los Angeles she accepted a teaching position in nearby Artesia.

In the summer of 1897, Lum moved east to Shenandoah, Iowa, a midwestern community where she associated with radical Holiness leader Charles Hanley and his World's Faith Missionary Association (WFMA), a communal Holiness group of fifty residents who resided in two plainly furnished faith homes. The community shared chores that sustained their life together, eating meals of plain food and participating in worship and Bible study three times a day. In the summer of 1898, while involved with WFMA, Lum was sanctified through a "powerful spiritual experience," which she later described in these words:

"Thank God for deliverance from all sin, through the precious Blood. I had been sanctified and anointed with the Holy Ghost years ago."[1]

Fairly soon after coming to Shenandoah, Lum started writing for the WFMA's newsletter, *The Firebrand,* and by 1899, Hanley, who referred to her as the "Lord's handmaiden especially adapted to this work,"[2] appointed her co-editor. By the next year, Lum had taken on additional responsibilities with Hanley's group. She was still serving as co-editor of the periodical, now known as *Missionary World,* which by that time was printing ten thousand copies monthly. Additionally, she agreed to serve as secretary, treasurer, and historian for the organization. During this period, Lum began preaching as an itinerating evangelist in neighboring communities. Along with these responsibilities, Lum found time to participate in local YWCA activities and became a leader in that organization, at one time representing the local chapter at the Iowa state convention.[3]

Still plagued by the same health problems that originally brought her to Los Angeles and bothered by the difficult Iowa winters, Lum went searching for a healthier climate. In the winter of 1904 she went to Salem, Oregon, where she worked in a rescue home and mission. Then, the winter of 1905 found her in Portland, assisting in another mission.

Finally, Lum was back in the Los Angeles area in spring of 1906 and began working as a stenographer for Phineas Bresee, one of the founders of the Church of the Nazarene. She had expected this to be a short-term position and was planning to return to Shenandoah to work with Hanley again. But in the interim, Lum encountered the Azusa Street Revival, and those plans changed.

When Clara Lum arrived at the Azusa Street Revival around May 1906, she had been "in the Lord's work for ten years" and came specifically seeking the baptism of the Holy Spirit. Though she had previously declared that she had been anointed by the Spirit as part of her sanctification, sometime before coming to

Azusa Street she was convinced that she had "grieved God and lost her experience [of sanctification]."⁴ She desired to receive the third work of grace as a confirmation that her sanctification had been retained or was restored. Shortly after coming to the revival, she had an encounter she later described in this way:

> When I came to Azusa Mission, I went in for the baptism with the Holy Ghost immediately. Had some digging to do, but the Lord met me. I was filled with the Holy Ghost many times and was shaken many times by the power of God. . . .
>
> But when I became a little child, clay in His hands, He baptized me with the Holy Ghost. At first He spoke just a few words through me. But recently He spoke different languages and sang songs in unknown tongues.⁵

Along with receiving the Holy Spirit baptism, Lum, like so many of the other early Pentecostal pioneers, reported receiving healing from the chronic condition that had brought her to Los Angeles in the first place and had plagued her for the years that she had been involved with the Holiness movement.

> Just lately the Lord healed me of quite a severe sickness. He has given me better health than ever, for which I thank Him. O, it was so sweet to have Him talk and sing through me when I was sick, during the night seasons. Sometimes I sang for hours and in a new voice and it did not tire me. He also interpreted. He said, "Jesus is coming." It rejoiced me so much, and then He sang a song right from heaven about His coming. O, praise God for the privilege of being in His work here.⁶

She also reported receiving the spiritual gifts of healing and casting out demons. Whether she ever used these gifts to minister or preach in the worship services at the Azusa Street Mission is unknown. Shortly, she became an integral part of the ministry of the Azusa Street Mission and Revival. Lum served as one of the six female members of the administrative board that initially oversaw the mission. Possibly, as part of that position, Lum accompanied Rachel Sizelove and a group of other saints to investigate the spot where Sizelove reported that God had shown her in a vision a camp meeting of in Arroyo Seco. The board's approval of the site set the stage for a string of events that eventually brought a revival—one that rivaled the Azusa Street meeting in size and spiritual enthusiasm.

In the worship services, Lum exercised the gifts of tongues and interpretation and read the testimonies of those who wrote to the mission. Outside the worship services, she was one of several people responsible for responding to the numerous letters the mission received daily. In this role, she not only had the task of corresponding with everyday supporters but also had the opportunity to exchange letters with leaders in the Holiness and Pentecostal movements and many more who would become leaders. Among those to whom Lum communicated was Thomas Barratt, who was to become the "apostle of the Pentecostal movement in Europe."

Dear Bro. Barratt in Christ:
. . . We were rejoiced beyond measure to read [your last letter]. I felt the power of God as I handled it and copied it off and edited it for the paper. Took it and read it to the saints and the power of God fell upon them as I read and one received the Pentecost and began speaking in tongues. It was brother G. B. Cashwell, a holiness preacher who came all the way from Dunn, N.C., to receive his Pentecost. He had been waiting on God for a few days and . . . in the meeting this afternoon the fire fell upon him as your letter was read. . . . We pray that God will mightily use you for you are a chosen vessel to carry this Gospel. . . .We want to hear from you often, we want to be one with you in prayer and in the blessed Spirit. May the Lord keep you humble and under the blood where he can glorify his name in signs and wonders . . . through you, that many may receive salvation and baptism with the Holy Ghost and healing.[7]

What was to make her indispensable to the phenomenal growth of the revival, however, was her skill in editing and administration that had proven so useful with Hanley and Bresee. This ability was invaluable for helping to get out word about the revival to a constituency eager to hear as much as possible about what God was doing. Her clerical and administrative skills allowed her, among other things, to record the messages in tongues given at the revival and set the stage for Lum to move into her most valuable position.

There is no doubt that Lum was, by nature and training, a gifted editor. After receiving the Pentecostal experience of Holy Spirit baptism, however, she was convinced that God had added a supernatural "anointing" for writing to her natural ability. It is possible that the initial idea to begin a newspaper chronicling the events of the Azusa Street Revival came from Lum, since she was the one person at Azusa Street who had seen firsthand how useful such a production could be and had the experience and ability to handle such an undertaking. Further, she had invaluable contacts with people in the Holiness community who could lend their assistance to such an endeavor. It was Lum, for example, who solicited Hanley and received the fifteen dollars to purchase a typewriter to produce the publication.[8]

In any event, Lum served as secretary and co-editor of the Azusa Street Mission's *Apostolic Faith* from 1906–8 and was integrally involved in every aspect of the newspaper. She wrote some articles and edited many, many more. She developed and maintained a mailing list that rapidly grew to more than twenty thousand names for local, national, and international constituencies and regularly oversaw the mailing of over five thousand copies of the organ on a more-or-less monthly basis. At its height, circulation reached forty thousand across the world and was distributed entirely free of charge, supported by offerings from the congregation and the recipients. Stories and testimonies of revival and healing poured in from every corner of the earth—Europe, Asia, Africa, and South America. Lum saw to it that the newspaper's readership got a feel for what was happening with the Azusa Street workers and the people whose lives they touched on every continent.

Lum was also responsible for recording some of Seymour's sermons in shorthand. Many of these found their way into *The Apostolic Faith*. It is because of her unique skills that some of the most graphic depictions of what was said and done at the revival have been preserved. Her portraits of the actual worship at the mission are some of the most descriptive. In an article entitled "Miss Clara Lum Writes Wonders," which appeared in the August 1906 issue of *Missionary World,* she wrote, "there is singing in the Spirit . . . the music is not learned. No one can join in unless it is given to them [by the Spirit]. They sing in different tongues at the same time, and the different parts are sung. Sometimes, one is singing in English, thus interpreting while the others are singing [in tongues]."[9]

Attestation to her editing skills and acknowledgment of her involvement in producing the newspaper came from a variety of places. Those who had worked with her at *Missionary World* said that she was "one of the most earnest and efficient workers and members" of their community. Glenn Cook, the mission's former business manager who later became a leader in the oneness Pentecostal movement, called her a "wonderful helper" in editing the paper.[10]

The first issue of *Apostolic Faith* did not appear until several months after her revival, when Seymour took note of Lum's nine years of editorial experience and enlisted her to work with him and Florence Crawford on the project. The three worked closely together on a regular basis, and their working relationship eventually blossomed into a deep friendship. Lum and Crawford became close during this period, possibly because, along with working together on the newsletter, they shared an interest and experience in rescue home work. But apparently Lum's and Seymour's relationship had a deeper quality to it. Reportedly, both had entertained the idea that the friendship could grow into a relationship that might result in marriage. However, when Seymour consulted his friend, Charles Harrison Mason, founder of the Church of God in Christ, about the possibility of marrying Lum, Mason cautioned him that such a marriage between a black man and a white woman would be very controversial and could lead to disaster for the ministry.[11] It is not surprising then that she, like Crawford, objected to Seymour's decision to marry Jennie Evans Moore. After the marriage, Lum left the mission. She never married.

As was often the case, all but a few of the articles Lum contributed to *The Apostolic Faith* were unsigned, as were many others. Exhibiting the modesty of many early Pentecostal, Seymour insisted that the newspaper's publication was a group effort and no individual, including himself, could take credit for any part of its publication. Yet Lum's stylistic signature was evident in several items appearing in the periodical. A number of articles appeared almost concurrently and with very little alteration in other publications. Take for example an item that appeared in the November 1906 issue of *Missionary World*:

The meetings have been running six months now. They begin at ten o'clock in the morning and hardly stop until twelve at night.[12]

An item with almost identical wording appeared the same month in *The Apostolic Faith*:

But here you find a mighty Pentecostal revival going on from ten o'clock in the morning till about twelve at night.[13]

The last edition of *The Apostolic Faith* that Lum helped Seymour produce from Los Angeles was the June 1908 issue, published a month after Seymour married Moore and the same month that Lum moved back to Oregon. Her reason for choosing Portland may have been twofold. First, her close relationship with Florence Crawford meant that Crawford's newly formed organization was a ready-made place for Lum to work.

Secondly, Lum still had relatives in that city. By 1908, her brother and her sister both lived there. Once Lum relocated to Portland, however, she lived in no fewer than fifteen locations.

With her move to Oregon, Lum corroborated with Crawford in taking *The Apostolic Faith*'s national and international mailing lists, leaving Seymour with only the small Los Angeles list. Within one month, she was working with Crawford, and the two continued publishing the newspaper, producing the July–August 1907 edition with no indication to the reading public that a substantial change had been made or that Seymour was no longer affiliated.[14] Their short disclaimer simply said, "We have moved the paper which the Lord laid on us to begin at Los Angeles to Portland, Oregon, which will now be its headquarters."[15]

Lum's importance in the regular production of the newspaper at either location cannot be overstated. Most historians suggest that its publication at Azusa Street was thwarted simply because Lum and Crawford were in possession of the mailing lists. It may also have been that the technical skill needed to produce the newspaper resided in Lum, and once she moved, Seymour was simply unable to find anyone with the competence to produce a regular periodical of the same caliber.

At any rate, after several months of the newspaper being published in Oregon, Lum and Crawford finally were ready to admit that the periodical they were publishing was not a continuation of the Azusa Street effort but an entirely new endeavor. "We said it was moved from Los Angeles," they wrote, "when we should have stated we were starting a new Apostolic Faith in Portland. . . ."[16] The Seymours went to Portland and tried, without success, to get Lum and Crawford to return the mailing lists.

When Crawford established her new organization, Lum served as editor of the children's newspaper. She also worked as a teacher in the Apostolic Faith School. While working with Crawford, Lum continued to file stories to *Missionary World* until at least 1910. She had also contributed to the December 1907 issue of the *Bridegroom Messenger*.

For the remainder of her life, Lum associated with Crawford's Apostolic Faith. For most of that time, she worked behind the scenes at the organization's headquarters, and presumably continued itinerant evangelistic preaching. But we hear nothing more of her for thirty-six years. Lum died in Gresham, Oregon, near Portland, in 1946 at the age of seventy-seven.

PART THREE

From Azusa Street to the World

One hallmark of genuine revival is a renewed zeal for missions—a passionate desire to spread the newly rekindled faith to those who have become complacent or who have never heard. The Azusa Street Revival certainly exemplified such zeal as it not only attracted many women and men with a long history of involvement in missions, but it also launched many more missionaries, who had experienced and desired to proclaim its particular brand of Holy Ghost fired renewal. Women made up a substantial number of those who went out from Azusa Street to every corner of the globe, taking with them the message of Pentecostal revival. They served not only as team members but also as leaders of these expeditions.

Almost immediately, teams went throughout the United States. They first covered the West Coast going through the cities and towns of California, Oregon, and Washington. They then went to the Midwest—Minnesota, Illinois, Missouri, and Ohio, then to the Northeast—to New York and Pennsylvania—and to the South—Virginia, Louisiana, and Texas. Wherever they found hungry hearts who invited them into the congregation, they testified and preached about their own experience and the biblical foundations on which it stood, and prayed with folks for salvation, sanctification, Holy Spirit baptism, and divine healing. When they had no invitation, they made do by preaching in the streets, putting up tents, borrowing buildings from whoever *would allow them. They stayed for as little as a few days and as long as several months, depending entirely on the leading of the Spirit and the reception of their message. And often they left new fledgling Pentecostal congregations behind.*

Women as well as men withstood the disdain of institutional churches, even among their Holiness brethren. The ecstatic worship in their meetings—the singing, shouting, tongues, and all manners of manifestations—regularly drew the attention and the derision of the local press. For though reporters often dismissed these meetings as the curious doings of a strange sect, they considered these antics a sensational drawing card that would capture their readers' eyes. Women as well as men faced the fierce anger of neighbors and local entrepreneurs whose peace they disturbed and business they disrupted. They, too, endured the violence of mobs and the risk of being jailed or run out of town.

Yet the hardships they suffered in the States could not compare with what they and their colleagues were to face on foreign soil. Leaving the relative safety of this country, they ventured to South America, Europe, Africa, and Asia and experienced strange customs, harsh traveling conditions, meager accommodations, illness, and death. Many heard the call through dialects that they identified as native to the land. Many believed that they were especially endowed with the ability to preach the gospel in native tongues without the aid of study or an interpreter. In most cases this was to prove untrue, but with the fire of Azusa Street burning in them, they remained undaunted and steadfast in their determination to take the Pentecostal message to the uttermost parts of the earth.

They went by faith, making up their fare as they traveled by train or steamer from meeting to meeting, accepting whatever offerings God placed on the hearts of their hearers to give. Yet through all the hardship and with meager means, they felt genuinely fortunate to be counted worthy to take the Pentecostal message to a world in need of revival. They praised God that they had been allowed to suffer for the sake of the gospel.

chapter 5

Florence Reed Crawford

PERHAPS THE WOMAN FROM AZUSA STREET who most influenced the Pentecostal movement beyond the initial period of revival was Florence Crawford. Though she was not a member of the original group that moved from the Bonnie Brae Street prayer meeting to Azusa Street, Crawford rapidly rose to a position of trust and importance and served in a variety of ministries at the mission for a short term. Within several months, she had begun to travel extensively and, within little more than one year, had a breach with Seymour, left Azusa Street, and planted a church that shortly grew into a denomination.

Florence Reed was one of six children, having three brothers and two sisters. Despite her atheist and free-thinking parents, she appeared to have an early interest in spiritual things. As a youngster, she reports evidence of two particular incidences of interest. Without permission as a child, she went to a camp meeting where a gospel message was being delivered and was deeply touched by the singing of the hymn, "Oh, the Bleeding Lamb."

On another occasion, probably when she was a young teen, her family hosted a famous free-thinker for a lecture. Florence was asked to sing a solo and chose to sing "Jesus, Lover of my Soul." By the time she finished her selection, several in attendance were in tears, having been visibly moved by the fervor with which she sang. At that time, however, she had not yet made a confession of Christian faith.

Despite poor health, Florence had a normal and active young life and enjoyed the regular social activities of girls her age. She attended social events with her friends, frequented theaters, hosted card parties, and engaged in ballroom dancing. In the midst of this active social life, her Christian experience began dramatically and seemingly came out of nowhere. She had a direct confrontation with God in what would seem to be a very unlikely place: a ballroom dance floor. She recalled the episode:

> One night as I was dancing in a ballroom I heard a voice speak out of Heaven and say "Daughter, give Me thine heart." I did not know it was the voice of God so I went on dancing. Again the voice spoke. It seemed my feet became heavy and the place was no longer beautiful to me. Again the voice spoke much louder, "Daughter, give Me thine heart!" The music died away and I left the ballroom; and for three days and nights I prayed and wept, wrestling against the powers of atheism and darkness. The enemy would tell me there was no God, and that the Bible was a myth. I could hardly eat or sleep, and it seemed there was no hope for me, but I thought: Why did God speak out of Heaven if there were no hope?
>
> At last I remembered a woman I knew was a Christian, and I went to her home. When she opened the door and looked at my face she said, "You want God." I said, "I want Him more than anything else in the world." Right there I fell on my knees, and as she prayed for me, God came into my heart."[1]

Florence came to Los Angeles in 1890 at the age of eighteen.

In that same year she married building contractor Frank Mortimer Crawford. The marriage was not particularly successful, and the couple separated around 1907. Before separating, they had two children—a daughter, Mildred, born in 1897, and a son, Raymond, born in 1891. They also adopted another child, a girl named Virginia.

After coming to California, Crawford involved herself in social work and in the leadership of women's organizations. She served a term as state president of the Los Angeles chapter of the Women's Christian Temperance League and became the first president of the Los Angeles chapter of the National Congress of Mothers, which later became the Parent-Teacher Association (PTA).

Around the same time, Crawford embarked on a search for the vital spiritual environment in which her newfound faith could take root and grow. This search led her to move from flock to flock, at various times affiliating with Methodist, Christian, and Missionary Alliance, and Presbyterian congregations. What she was ultimately looking for was the experience of sanctification. She was generally discouraged from seeking any further experience or witness of sanctification and was exhorted to accept, by faith, that she had received it. Such exhortation did not curb Crawford's desire for an inner witness, so she continued her attempt to find a group of people who wholeheartedly embraced the teaching of a definite witness of the experience.

Her pursuit finally led to Azusa Street during the early days of the revival. There she encountered the spirited singing of the saints, as sanctified people referred to themselves. Before a word was preached, Crawford was met by a chorus of Hallelujahs that she later testified, "went through my soul, as [I] thought, 'God, I have heard from heaven.'"[2]

Soon after coming to Azusa Street, Crawford received the Pentecostal experience of tongues. Along with the ability to speak, she reportedly engaged in writing in seven or eight different languages. With her baptism, she also reported instantaneous healing from an assortment of ailments that had plagued her for a number of years: A childhood bout with spinal meningitis left her with poor eyesight; a throw from a carriage as a teen left her wearing surgical supports for her back; an episode of tuberculosis left her with a variety of lung problems, including a chronic cough and hemorrhaging. Though she had worn glasses for some time, she regained perfect eyesight. She recounts the miraculous healing that affected her entire body:

> I had many afflictions on my body, but I never once thought of praying for the healing of my body until God baptized me with the Holy Ghost and fire. I had worn glasses for years. Three attacks of spinal meningitis early in my life had left my head and eyes so affected that I could not leave the glasses off. I went to the mission that afternoon and told what wonderful things the Lord had done for me. As I had them pray; the healing power of the Son of God flowed through my eyes, and my eyes were perfect. I had lung trouble for years and had to live in southern California for my health, but God healed me of that. I was thin, diseased, broken down in every part of my body, but when I had paid the full price and in simple, childlike faith prayed that I might get my health back again and be a witness for Him in this world, the healing streams began to flow.[3]

Crawford was one of six women who served on the Azusa Street administrative board. During the worship services, she could be found working at the altar, praying with those who needed healing or wanted salvation, sanctification, or the baptism of the Holy Spirit. She also served as co-editor (along with Seymour and Clara Lum) of *The Apostolic Faith* newsletter and was second only to Seymour in the number of signed articles contributed to the periodical. She possibly wrote many more since a great deal of the articles were unsigned. She was instrumental in distributing the monthly newspaper that chronicled the events of the revival to Seymour's supporters. The extent of her influence among the revival constituents can be attested to in later editions of the newsletter. She, like Seymour, had resorted to using only her initials to sign articles. Presumably, everyone knew who F.L.C. was.

Dreams and visions were a regular phenomenon in the Pentecostal culture of Azusa Street, and Crawford was known for having visions that she often relayed in a testimony service or to the readers of *The Apostolic Faith*. An article in the newspaper recounted one such vision: "While Sister Crawford was praying [for] money to send workers to Oakland, the Lord gave her a vision of three bills she would receive and she received three five dollar bills. Then when praying about her fare to Salem, Oregon, she saw three gold pieces and sure enough she received the gold pieces."[4]

Though she had no previously known preaching experience, her role in the leadership of women's organizations must have given her considerable experience in public speaking and attested to her skill at the art. She quickly became a gifted preacher with her newly found zeal through Holy Spirit baptism. Some credit her as the first of all the Azusa Street converts to take the Pentecostal message on the revival circuit. Beginning in Los Angeles, she moved through California, stopping in Oakland, where she and G.W. and May Evans conducted a five-week revival. In that meeting, "sixty-five souls received the baptism with the Holy Ghost, thirty were sanctified and nineteen converted."[5] Her nightly meetings drew overflow crowds with standing room only. Often seekers had to be turned away, and local law enforcement authorities had to be called to keep order. Even though she traveled extensively and was away from Azusa Street for long periods, her loyalty to the mission was explicit and unquestioned, for she wrote:

> There is no spot on earth so dear to me as this place, but I must go out and tell this story. Souls are perishing far and near. The Lord told me yesterday to go into all the world and preach His

Gospel. "The kingdom of heaven is at hand," and "Behold, I come quickly." What He says to me, He says to every baptized soul. He wants us to go out into the highways and hedges and declare this Gospel. He has anointed me to tell the story of Jesus and I can go alone for Jesus is with me. O, glory to God![6]

Like so many Azusa adherents, Crawford's ministry included the gift of healing and prayer. Divine healing was a regular part of the services she conducted. Crawford reported such a healing in her December 1906 meeting in Salem, Oregon. These healings were indicative of the regular supernatural experiences that the saints expected and received: "A cancer and a rupture of seven years standing have been healed in Salem since we got here. The cancer came out in three days, roots and all. Jesus is healing the sick. Many other healings are taking place."[7]

Perhaps in admiration of her administrative gifts, her loyalty, and her hard work, Seymour named her State Overseer of California and entrusted her to open new works throughout the state in the name of the Apostolic Faith Mission. During the remainder of 1906 and in early 1907, Crawford continued to direct teams of evangelists to hold revivals throughout California. Revivals were held in cities such as San Francisco, Oakland, San Jose, and Santa Rosa as well as principal cities of the Northwest, including Salem and Portland, Oregon and Seattle, Washington.

During the early years of her ministry, whether at worship or working on some ministry project, Florence was often accompanied by her daughter Mildred. The ten-year-old can be found seated in the official portrait of the early board. Some scholars believe that, even at this young age, Mildred served as part of the credentialing board. Evidence shows that she was an active participant in revival services and had had her own Pentecostal experience. She also traveled extensively with her mother to many evangelistic campaigns (while her older brother was left at home with his father). At one point, juvenile officials in Portland,

Oregon, attempted to take her away from her mother, accusing the elder Crawford of permitting her daughter to "roll around on the floor among Negroes and white men for a couple of hours every night."[8]

In December 1906 while in San Francisco, she wrote back to the Azusa Street Mission stating:

Such a meeting we had. I never saw such sweet unity of the Spirit testimony, healing, singing in the Holy Ghost, praying for the sick, and some receiving their Pentecost at the same time, and no confusion. Oh it was glorious and surely the Holy Ghost led the meeting. As I read the text or lesson about bridling the tongue, a dear brother that has been a power in mission work, healing the sick and preaching, said, "Pray for me now that my tongue may be bridled." The power came for prayer. I laid hands on him and he was baptized and spoke in such a clear language. Another preacher was baptized soon after. Oh God is working mightily! A man was completely healed of rupture of nine years' standing, last night. Oh how can we praise Him enough? A sister the first time in the meeting, was healed and anointed, went home and got her Pentecost the same night.[9]

A number of people who were to later become immersed in the ministry of Azusa Street first encountered the Pentecostal baptism at Crawford's hands. Adolpho de Rosa, a Portuguese Methodist minister who was a former Catholic priest from the Cape Verde Islands, received baptism in one of her Oakland meetings. Ardella Mead, the Methodist missionary to Angola, had Crawford, Seymour, and "another sister" lay hands on her in an Azusa revival. Crawford also prayed for the healing of May Evans, the first white woman to receive the Pentecostal experience at Bonnie Brae Street.

As requests came in from *The Apostolic Faith* readers and those who witnessed her preaching in various meetings, Crawford's ministry carried her as far east as Minnesota and on to Canada. It was while she was in Minneapolis that Crawford felt God directing her to establish the headquarters of a new ministry in Portland, Oregon.[10] This directive may not have been so clear, or she may not have been so willing to obey the voice of God had it not been for other circumstances that were unfolding in Crawford's ministry at that time.

Approximately a year after assuming a leadership role in the mission, a breach developed between Seymour and Crawford that signaled the beginning of a break in their relationship and the beginning of a new direction in Crawford's own ministry. The breach stemmed from three possible sources: First, Crawford held the radical understanding of Christ's imminent return shared by many early Pentecostals and, with it, the extreme position of some that such normal activities as marriage and raising a family were counterproductive to the urgent need to reach as many as possible with the Pentecostal message before Christ's return.

Secondly, since Crawford had held a somewhat prominent place in the ministry, she may have felt threatened by what the new alliance between Seymour and Moore could mean for her own leadership position. Lastly, Seymour had instituted a number of small but significant changes in the governmental structure of the Azusa Street Mission that effectively limited the level of leadership to which Crawford could ultimately rise. In developing a doctrinal statement for the mission, he made a clear distinction in the roles of men and women in vital areas of worship and ministry leadership, insisting that "all ordination must be done by men not women. Women may be ministers but not to baptize or ordain in this work."[11] The liturgy he created for the ordination service clearly indicated that all laying on of hands and prayer within such service was to be done by "elders."[12] This might suggest that already the levels of ministry to which women might aspire were somewhat restricted. Apparently the ranks of elder and bishop were restricted to men, with women relegated to lower ranks with fewer ministerial privileges.

Crawford made several trips to the Northwest alone and as head of evangelistic teams to conduct worship services and set churches in order. Though she maintained her affiliation with the Azusa Street Mission, Crawford was also setting some alliances in place that would serve her well should she decide to permanently relocate out of the state. In May 1908, Crawford left the Azusa Street Mission for the last time to move to Portland and set up her own Apostolic Faith Mission. Following her departure, Seymour instituted a second change that further lessened the impact of women's leadership at the mission. Though women had been members of the loosely organized early administrative board, the increasingly tighter structure put into place during latter years essentially excluded women in positions of authority. Four of the five people who served on the formal board of trustees that finally had legal responsibility for gover-nance of the mission were men. The only woman granted a posi-tion on that board was Seymour's wife, Jennie.

Shortly after Crawford's departure, Clara Lum left the Azusa Street Mission and joined her in Portland, bringing with her *The Apostolic Faith* mailing list and much of the expertise for pub-lishing the newspaper. Though the official account by Crawford's organization is that the Azusa Street ministry "turned over responsibility for publishing the newspaper," most sources suggest that Crawford's departure and moving of the list to Oregon was a much less cooperative venture. Seymour accused Crawford and Lum of removing the newsletter deceitful-ly. In a public account of the situation published in the October/November 1908 issue of *The Apostolic Faith*—the last issue he attempted to produce in Los Angeles, Seymour told the existing readership:

I must for the salvation of souls let it be known that the editor is still in Los Angeles and will not remove *The Apostolic Faith* from Los Angeles, without letting subscribers and field workers know.

This is a sad thing to our hearts for a worker to attempt to take the paper which is the property of the Azusa Street Mission to another city without consent after being told not to do so.[13]

Seymour made several attempts to get the mailing list back from Crawford but failed. Reportedly, the relationship between the two remained contentious for several years, with Seymour making at least one failing attempt to gain control of Crawford's entire work.

No matter how or why Crawford left the Azusa Street group, she was to have her greatest impact after she departed. In June 1907, Crawford was ready to hold her first Portland camp meeting in a borrowed sanctuary. But her aggressive outreach campaigns soon netted a larger following, and the ministry grew quickly. Within a year, Crawford had acquired facilities that included two auditoriums with a combined seating of more than three thousand. Her interest, however, was not in attracting a large membership, and she maintained no formal membership roll for her congregations or the resulting denomination.

By July 1908, Crawford made Portland the international publishing headquarters for *The Apostolic Faith* newspaper. During the interim period, Crawford and Lum had continued to publish the newspaper but without disclosing to the readership that it had been moved and removed from Seymour's tutelage. Now they openly announced that the periodical had moved and was under new direction.

Besides becoming an excellent preacher, Crawford was to become a prolific songwriter, composing several hymns for her organization. After her death, these were collected along with several written by her son and daughter into a denominational hymnal. Many of these hymns dealt with classic Holiness/Pentecostal themes. Some, however, covered exotic subjects that demonstrated the distinctive tenets of Crawford's brand of Pentecostalism.

For in addition to the mainline Holiness Pentecostal tenets, including strictures concerning women wearing worldly apparel and facial make-up or having bobbed hair, Crawford added several elements less popular or uniquely her own. Like Seymour and some others, she insisted that remarried divorcees separate from each other before being involved in the church. She refused to take a collection during the worship services. But Crawford held even more extreme ideas on religion. She generally frowned on marriage, counseled young people to stay single, and encouraged celibacy even among married people.[14] She denounced advocates of "finished work" theology as termed by William Durham.

One of Crawford's closest allies in ministry was her son Raymond Robert Crawford, who was ordained in 1910 at the age of nineteen. From that time on, he served as his mother's assistant overseer and traveled with her on evangelistic tours. After her death, he succeeded her as general overseer. By then her daughter Mildred had taken on a less-visible role in the ministry, serving primarily as a musician.

Called "Mother" by her followers, Crawford was reportedly heavy-handed in her leadership style, and her organization was extremely sectarian—to the point that she forbade members to participate in worship even with other Pentecostal bodies. Perhaps for that reason, the denomination never grew to more than forty-two congregations during her lifetime. The rigidly centralized authority of the Portland headquarters required all pastors to come to Portland every summer for the three month tent meeting. During these sessions, Crawford preached her "militant" gospel message and expounded on the doctrines of the Apostolic Faith Mission. Many pastors saw their absence as a hardship on their fledgling congregations that were left to fend for themselves.

Crawford's leadership of the Apostolic Faith Mission did not go completely unchallenged. In 1919, when the undercurrent of discontent gave way to a full-fledged confrontation, a group of male evangelists split off from the organization to form a new organization, the Bible Standard Mission.[15] We cannot overlook the fact that many male pastors who served under Crawford held some resentment. Females dominated the organization from the very beginning. At the very first conference, the majority decided that "women (other than Crawford, of course) could preach, but not lead."[16]

Crawford died in 1936 at the age of sixty-four. The greatest strength of her Apostolic Faith Mission lies outside the U.S., with more than 122 churches around the world. While there are only fifty congregations in the United States, there are fifteen congregations in Nigeria, eleven in Canada, nineteen in Asia, eight in Europe, seventeen in the West Indies, and two in Australia.

chapter 6

Lucy Leatherman

L UCY M. LEATHERMAN WAS ONE of the true mission-ary pioneers of the Azusa Street Revival. The widow of a physician, Leatherman was probably among the revival's most educated women. We have absolutely no information on her early life except that she was born near Greencastle, Indiana, located in the west-central area of the state.

Her contribution to the early Pentecostal missions is distinc-tive in many ways. She traveled the farthest and most often to spread the message of Pentecostalism. Her ministry touched four continents and more than ten countries, landing her in capitals and remote cities with exotic names and cultures. She was unquestionably one of the most widely traveled persons—either man or woman—to go out from the mission.

She was unique among the women of the Azusa Street Revival in a number of ways. First, she often traveled alone as a single woman to countries where women were regularly relegated to second-class status and limited in their mobility and activities.

She endured incredible hardship, going by primitive means to remote locations. Lucy was fully engaged in the culture of the societies to which she ministered, often dressing in native clothing. She exposed herself to the rigors of extreme weather and comparatively uncomfortable accommodations along with the possibility of violence at the hands of robbers that terrorized the surrounding terrain.

Leatherman was also the most prolific of those women who filed reports of the spread of the revival to believers on both the American and European continents. She regularly contributed not only to the mission's *Apostolic Faith* but also to Alexander Boddy's *Confidence,* published in England; the *Church of God Evangel* in Tennessee; and *The Pentecost,* published by J. Roswell Flowers in Indianapolis. Along with contributing articles of various lengths to *Confidence,* Leatherman was instrumental in distributing the newsletter wherever she settled.

Throughout her ministry, Leatherman associated with several of the male leaders of both the Holiness and Pentecostal movements. Sometime around the turn of the century she had been affiliated with Parham's ministry in Topeka, Kansas. She had visited his Bible school and had become a close associate.[1] Sometime before 1904, she affiliated with Charles Hanley's World's Faith Missionary Association in Shenandoah, Iowa.

Evidence regarding her participation in the actual revival is scant, and her ties to the mission come primarily from her travels with the missionary teams and the reports she wrote in *The Apostolic Faith*. It is not certain just when or how she got to the Azusa Street Mission, but possibly she came on an invitation from Lucy Farrow, who had met her in an earlier meeting. We do not know how long she stayed at the meeting, but she traveled regularly as part of the missionary teams that went out from the revival.

Leatherman was one of those who reported having the gift of xenolalia and the ability to speak Arabic. Although it is questionable how extensively she was able to use this gift on the mission field, *The Apostolic Faith* reports an incident that occurred while she was ministering in Oakland.

> Sister Leatherman speaks the Turkish language, and while in Oakland, some were talking on the street about the gift of tongues. Sister Leatherman began to speak just as a man wearing the Turkish fez came by. He listened in wonder and asked what college she had attended, saying she spoke the most perfect Turkish tongue he had heard spoken by a foreigner. He was an educated man from a Turkish college in Constantinople. She told him the Holy Ghost gave her the language which she did not understand herself and he was the first person that had interpreted for her.[2]

Leatherman's missionary ministry covered a period beginning in 1906 and lasting until nearly 1923, when she returned to the United States from Argentina. Like many others, the first two years of her ministry were in the United States. By fall of 1906, as she was preparing to go to Jerusalem, Leatherman led a team with Louisa Condit and Andrew Johnson that traveled across the United States by way of the Northwest. They first traveled to Oakland, California; then to Colorado Springs and Denver, Colorado, to hold meetings. Finally, they arrived in Greenwich, Connecticut. There she worked with Ophelia Wiley and Adolpho de Rosa to conduct evangelistic campaigns. Often these meetings exhibited such spiritual fervor that they drew complaints from neighbors and the attention of local law enforcement. They were also victimized by angry mobs who tore down and torched the tent in which they were meeting. After being accused of witchcraft and hypnotism, the revival was over when Leatherman declared, "We will no longer work further in this locality."[3]

She stopped last in New York where she became involved in a revival meeting held by Maud Williams. One of the people she invited to those meetings was Thomas Ball Barratt, the

Norwegian Holiness leader. Barratt received his Pentecostal experience when Leatherman responded to his request to lay hands on him and pray. The need to have a woman lay hands on him caused Barratt a good deal of discomfort, which he attributed to a Satanic attempt to keep him from receiving his Pentecostal experience. Subsequently Barratt returned to Norway to share his testimony of the experience and to minister the message of Pentecostal Spirit baptism. His ministry sparked a revival throughout Norway and several other European countries. Barratt was only one of the early leaders to benefit from her gift of laying on of hands for the impartation of Holy Spirit baptism.

Leatherman's concern to establish a work in New York City was instrumental in the founding of Glad Tidings Tabernacle. Shortly after visiting New York, Leatherman wrote to Charles Parham, who had gone to Zion City, Illinois, to ask him to send someone to the city to establish a work there. Because of her efforts, Parham sent another woman, Marie Burgess, to New York to plant a church. Burgess was to become an important figure in Pentecostal history, and her church, Glad Tidings Tabernacle, became the largest Pentecostal congregation on the east coast for a number of years.

Leatherman's heart's desire, however, was to serve in foreign missions, and it was toward that goal that she was moving. The November 1906 *Apostolic Faith* carried excerpts from a longer testimony Leatherman had submitted with the disclaimer that "[w]e have not space for a full report":

> While seeking for the Baptism with the Holy Ghost in Los Angeles, after Sister Ferrell [sic] laid hands on me, I praised and praised God and saw my Savior in the heavens. And as I praised, I came closer and closer, and I was so small. By and by I swept into the wound in His side, and He was not only in me but I in Him, and there I found that rest that passeth all understanding,

and He said to me, you are in the bosom of the Father. He said I was clothed upon and in the secret place of the Most High. But I said, Father, I want the gift of the Holy Ghost, and the heavens opened and I was overshadowed, and such power came upon me and went through me. He said, Praise Me, and when I did, angels came and ministered unto me. I was passive in His hands, and by the eye of faith I saw angel hands working on my vocal cords, and I realized they were loosing me. I began to praise Him in an unknown language.

In a few days, while on my way to church, I met a lady and two little children. She was talking to her children in a language that sounded like the words God had given me. I spoke a sentence to her, and she said, "What you say means God has given Himself to you." She is from Beirut, Syria, and speaks Arabic. Eight years ago, in A. B. Simpson's missionary school at Nyack, New York, I heard the Macedonian cry to go to Jerusalem, but it is to the Arabs. I am told there are more Arabs than Jews there, and God has been speaking to me and asks me if I would be willing to go with Him to the wild Arab of the desert. Anywhere with Jesus I will gladly go. On land or sea, what matter where. Where Jesus is 'tis heaven there.

Pray that God will send a revival to this city and pray for Arabia.[4]

Leatherman's international travels began in 1907. These earliest trips were as an unaffiliated itinerant missionary, supported principally by faith offerings collected in the various revival meetings in which she ministered but with "no board in back of me."[5] She later affiliated with the Church of God (Cleveland, Tennessee), and received some monetary support from that organization.

By January 1907, Leatherman arrived in Assiout, Egypt, to help in a mission work and revival. She reported on the results of this revival and on withstanding harsh conditions, living outdoors in tents and traveling across the desert in the hot sun and cold evenings. In a short article entitled "Apostolic Revival in Egypt" she states:

> Magnify the Lord with me for the great revival in Egypt. Multitudes have been saved, sanctified and baptized with the Holy Ghost, and fire. We have out-grown our mission rooms and must live out-doors. God willing, as soon as the missionaries arrive from America, I go to new fields of labor as He opens the way. I believe Arabia will be where my Father will send me next. Pray for me.[6]

By May, Leatherman was in Palestine, in the city of Jerusalem, and sent a second shorter testimony to *Apostolic Faith*. It was published in a short article in the May 1907 edition, simply titled "Jerusalem":

> One native minister of Beyroute, Syria, came to Jerusalem to spend the winter. God has baptized him with the Holy Ghost and he speaks with tongues. Praise God! God started this movement in A.D. 32 in this dear old city, and the "latter rain" is falling in 1908. Glory to God! Miss Elizabeth Brown of the Christian and Missionary Alliance received her baptism more than two weeks ago. She had the real old-fashioned manifestations like many had at Azusa Street.—The secret of the matter was she was so given up to God. Praise His name! She came to my room and requested me to lay bands on her for her baptism. She felt waves of fire passing through her head and face and then began to speak in tongues. She sings the heavenly chant. It is precious to hear her.
>
> Lucy M. Leatherman, Jerusalem, Palestine, care of American consulate.[7]

In August 1908, *The Apostolic Faith* reported that Leatherman was in Jerusalem again. By December, she had gone on to Beirut, Lebanon, and several cities of the Sinai, where she was involved in conducting revival services. From there, she went on to Galilee in Nazareth, then to Assiout, Egypt, where she visited a missionary acquaintance.

By January 1909, Leatherman was reporting on the revival meeting in Egypt. The response was so big to the work there that the group outgrew its facilities and was forced to move outside. At the time she was making plans to go to Arabia.

Leatherman spent the summer of that same year in Shanghai, China, and Japan. As she prepared to leave Japan, she filed a short testimony to the Pentecost, asking for prayer that God would send additional workers to start missionary work in Russia and Turkey, as well as Syria and Palestine. At the time, she was making plans to return to the United States for a period of rest but was looking forward to returning to Jerusalem. She was also planning to start her own newsletter and was looking for someone to edit the periodical. Whether she ever did this is unknown, as there are no known extant issues.[8]

In this short testimony, an interest toward the ministry of women surfaced. Though Leatherman was often at the forefront of ministry "treading the winepress," she felt that men were more suited to leadership and stated emphatically, "God is calling for men to go to the forefront of the battle. Mary ran and told Peter and the disciples that Christ had risen, but men were always at the head of things, men of honest report and filled with the Holy Ghost. Praise God!"[9]

February 1910 found Leatherman in Manila, the Philippines, to which she referred as "this wicked city" and where she ministered to soldiers and sailors. She wrote the staff of *Confidence* magazine to solicit literature and Bibles to distribute in her work there.[10]

In August 1912, Leatherman was visiting Kafushima in Syria. There she faced a new danger—the possible invasion by the French and Italians. It was here that Leatherman's reports exhibited their distinction from her colleagues, not just in their volume but in the breadth of detail she provided. Her correspondences showed that she was as much aware of the political and social realities of the countries in which she served as she was with their perceived spiritual need and the revival that was breaking out around her. She wrote, "The French are coming to take charge of the Lebanon Mount, and are to appoint a new pasha. Also, the Italians are at the Dardanelles, and we cannot tell what a day may bring forth."[11]

Leatherman returned to the Middle East in 1914 to visit Egypt and Palestine. In 1916 she returned to the United States for a short period and joined the Church of God, affiliating with a congregation in Valdosta, Georgia. She had learned about the denomination from other missionaries while in Egypt and Palestine. In December she boarded a steamer ship and sailed down the west coast of South America to Buenos Aires, Argentina. This time she traveled as a Church of God missionary, with the support of $532 that had been provided by the General Assembly. During her trip, she periodically stopped in several ports in Peru and for a longer time in Chile. In undertaking this trip, Leatherman also holds the distinction of being one of the earliest missionaries to go out from the Church of God.

Leatherman was in Peru for only a short time and stopped at each port only a few days, yet she was determined to make the most of the opportunity. In each port she personally witnessed to as many souls as possible. Presumably, she also stopped on her return trip to the States and engaged in the same pattern of witnessing. Though she was the first Church of God missionary to reach that country, she did not attempt to start a permanent work in Peru. According to Charles Conn in *Where the Saints Have Trod,* "This effort was so limited that no results were noted."[12]

Disembarked in Valparaiso, Chile, in May 1917, Leatherman became the first Church of God missionary to reach that nation. When she arrived, however, she found an established and seemingly thriving Pentecostal work under the auspices of H. C. Hoover and the Methodist Pentecostal Church with about four hundred members. The Pentecostal revival had started in that nation around the same time that the outpouring had begun in Los Angeles. Leatherman was so impressed with this work that she spent several months in Valparaiso, Santiago, and several surrounding communities, preaching in the revival meetings of existing Pentecostal groups. She left Chile in August 1917 and began a journey over the Andes to Argentina.

In Argentina, Leatherman joined F. L. Ryder and his wife, who were also missionaries from the Church of God. The trio worked together in this country for five years supported by denominational funding. Their headquarters was in Herado, a suburb four miles outside of Buenos Aires. They established missions in Herado and Ramos Mejia, set up two Sunday schools, and erected a building presumably for worship. Apparently, their hard work bore little lasting fruit, for when they returned to the United States in 1923, little remained of their efforts in this area. Regretfully, here, too, ends the trail for information on Leatherman. It was not until several years later that a permanent Church of God congregation was established in Argentina. Yet the denomination credits Leatherman for her groundbreaking work in that country.

chapter 7

Ophelia Wiley

O F ALL THE WOMEN WHO VENTURED forth with the missionary teams from Azusa Street, we know least about Ophelia Wiley. We have no knowledge of when she was born, where she was born, where she spent her childhood years, the level of her early educational attainment, or the depth of her early spiritual experience. We have no access to extant photographs of her and have no idea what she looked like except that she was described as a mulatto or quadroon—a light-skinned black woman whom one article referred to as "that yellow girl from Los Angeles."[1]

The reports that we have depict her as a powerful preacher who made at least two missionary trips from Azusa Street. Wiley was considered a "'star singer' who stood in the middle of the spotlight most of the time."[2] She was also a songwriter, and many of the numbers she sang were her own compositions.

The only description of her in the Apostolic Faith says that she was one of a party of seven—"a band of Spirit-filled workers"[3] who went out from the mission to the Northwest. This group, led by Florence Crawford, traveled on the evangelistic circuit by steamer ship to Northern California and throughout the Northwest, stopping first in Oakland then going on to Salem, Oregon, and Seattle, Washington. The others included G. W. and May Evans, Brother and Sister Thomas Junk, Brother and Sister C. W. Solkeld, and Lulu Miller.

The team worked under Crawford's direction as state director, except for a short period. When Crawford was summoned back to Los Angeles to assist in some aspect of the work there, the group stayed in the Northwest and continued to hold revival meetings in which they preached, taught, and testified of their Pentecostal experience at Azusa Street.

Wiley and Miller were black. The remainder of the group was white; according to Larry Martin, their traveling and ministering together represented an attempt to export the apparent racial equality and unity of the Azusa Street Revival beyond its own doors.[4]

These meetings became outpost centers of Pentecostal ministry and mission, rivaling the spiritual fervor in Los Angeles. They regularly drew overflowing crowds of people from the surrounding towns and villages who could not or did not want to travel the distance to Los Angeles to attend the Azusa Street meetings but longed to meet and hear from those who had been there. They paralleled those meetings not only in the frequency of Holy Spirit baptism but also for the occurrence of miraculous episodes of divine healing, demonic deliverance, and demonstrations of spiritual exuberance. For example, during their Salem campaign, Wiley joined Crawford and other members of their company to pray for a blind woman who was instantaneously healed. Such occurrences only fanned the flame of revival even hotter and drew even more attention to their home base at Azusa Street. And letters poured into *The Apostolic Faith* and other of the movement's periodicals from wherever teams went attesting to the supernatural character of these meetings.

Closer to Los Angeles, one could frequently find Ophelia Wiley among the Azusa Street faithful, who regularly held street services on whatever corner they could find available. Often within a community, their fervor caused as much discontent as spiritual excitement. One article in the *Los Angeles Times* demonstrates the fervor with which these adherents approached their felt commission to spread the gospel of Pentecost.

Psalms of Victory! Psalms of Victory! Yelled Mrs. [Ophelia] J. Wiley, a Negress . . . as she was lead from Second and Los Angeles Streets . . . to Central Station. In vain did the woman sing, yell and preach "holy rollerisms" to the patrolman, but it was all in vain.

Since the holy rollers left their abode on Azusa Street, a branch of the sect had been holding street meetings. Their fanatical preachings have so disturbed the neighborhood that the police were forced to take up the permit allowing them to preach. Although the officers attempted to reason with the woman, they found it impossible, as the woman continued to sing and pray. [She] was finally released.[5]

In another example, in September 1906, Wiley accompanied a group of missionaries bound for Africa to the train station. There she held forth with her usual religious enthusiasm, singing and preaching the gospel message and the reality of her newfound Pentecostal experience. Again, the resulting commotion ended with an arrest of one of her party:

For about two hours at the depot, the saints sang, while some wept and rejoiced in the Spirit, and some danced before the Lord. While Sister Wiley was preaching the Gospel to the crowd, one of the officials, being angry, tried to break up the meeting, but the saints began to pray, and were allowed to continue undisturbed for some time, till a brother began to speak in tongues. This seemed to stir the devil and Bro. Lee was put out into the street, which resulted in a meeting there. God has wonderfully supplied the means to send the missionaries.[6]

Despite her many gifts and the success of her meetings, Wiley contributed only one item to *The Apostolic Faith*. A "Sermon from a Dress," published in the October 1906 edition, demonstrates Wiley's understanding of salvation, sanctification, and Holy Spirit baptism:

The Lord makes His truth so plain that a wayfaring man, though a fool, shall not err therein. You have all seen a dirty dress washed. But you never saw a person take a dirty dress and iron it. And you never saw them take a dress and wash and iron it all at once. And you never saw a person put on a dress and iron it. The dirty dress represents a person in sin. Your righteousness is filthy rags. "Though your sins be as scarlet, they shall be as white as snow." When you get the dress washed, that represents a justified experience. When the dress is washed and on the line, you rejoice because the washing is through.

But the clothes need nothing else before they are ready to wear. What do they need? Why, they need to be ironed. You would be ashamed to take the clothes off the line and wear them without ironing. Jesus would be ashamed to present you before the Father if you were not sanctified, but when you are sanctified He is not ashamed to call you brethren. Christ gave Himself for His church that He might wash it and present it without spot or wrinkle. So we must let Him iron out all the wrinkles.

What next? You take an ironed garment and there is something lacking yet. What is it? Why you need to put it on and wear it. But that is no work. The work was done when you washed and ironed it. So the Holy Ghost is a free gift. It is the promise of the Father to the soul that is sanctified. You do not have to repent to get the Holy Ghost, but you must be washed clean and whiter than snow. Now you have nothing to mourn over, but something to rejoice over. You can know you are baptized. The Holy Ghost will cut your tongue loose and let you praise Him in an unknown language. God will not iron a dirty piece. He will take out the spots and then the wrinkles, and after these two weeks, He will baptize you with His free gift—the Holy Ghost.[7]

Wiley arrived in Salem, Oregon, in November 1906, one month before Florence Crawford could join her and break away from her many responsibilities as state field director, co-editor of

The Apostolic Faith, and member of the Azusa Street administrative board. Though Wiley was considered a leader in the group, presumably she was accompanied by Lulu Miller, and their task was to hold down the fort and conduct services until Crawford could get to the city. Reports in the Pentecostal press spoke glowingly of the meetings:

> The work here is progressing gloriously, although the opposition is deep and bitter. Two days ago in the preliminary service in the prayer tower, the "upper room," Sister Ryan received her personal Pentecost. She spoke in tongues for nearly three quarters of an hour without intermission. It was the most astonishing case we have had yet in this city. Everyone that saw it was amazed and strengthened in their faith. She spoke in at least seven languages. Glory to Jesus!
> The whole city and country round about are being shaken.[8]

As in Los Angeles, stories of these meetings made excellent filler for the local papers of the towns to which they traveled. For example, in December 1906, newspapers around Salem, Oregon, carried several stories of the "antics" of Crawford, Wiley, and their group in that area.[9] They were less favorable than the religious organs. In speaking specifically of Wiley, for instance, the *Daily Capitol Journal* wrote, "Unless one counts a senseless piece of doggerel by Sister Wiley as coming direct from the Holy Spirit, nothing was handed down at the meeting in this Pentecostal mission on Twelfth Street."[10]

Like her comrades, Wiley was a woman of strong faith who lived in the heady environment of the new movement in which people were led entirely by the Holy Spirit to do extraordinary things. Often these actions made little or no apparent sense to skeptics in the more learned religious community. On one occasion Wiley was led to go to Seattle, although she knew no one in the city. Once she arrived, she was led further to a specific house. When she rang the bell, a woman answered and informed her that she had been praying for God to send someone to her home. Wiley responded, "I'm a missionary and the Holy Ghost sent me to Seattle."[11] Obviously, Wiley was there to minister to a specific need of which she was previously unaware.

Like so many of the other women who went out from Azusa Street, we lose track of Wiley at this point.

chapter 8

Lillian Anderson Garr

A MONG THE COUPLES
ASSOCIATED with the
Azusa Street Mission,
perhaps none was better
known or had a greater impact
on the development of early
Pentecostal missions than
Alfred Garrison (A. G.) Garr
and his wife Lillian. For several
years before coming to Azusa
Street, the Garrs worked as
evangelists and church planters
for the Hanley's World's Faith
Missionary Association. This
missionary association, also
known as the Burning Bush
Organization, was the radical
Holiness group that was head-
quartered in Shenandoah,
Iowa. So by the time the Garrs came to Azusa Street, they already
had made somewhat of a name for themselves as revivalists
throughout a large portion of the United States.

We know a great deal more about Lillian's ministry than
many of the other women, not only because of the correspon-

dences the Garrs filed back to the Azusa Street Mission or other Pentecostal periodicals, but also because after Lillian's premature death and her husband's long and successful ministry, Alfred caught the attention of several Pentecostal historians. In telling his story, they give us glimpses into Lillian's life and ministry. Still, these are only glimpses of a woman who was a powerful preacher and teacher in her own right. Frank Ewart, an early Pentecostal leader, referred to her as "one of the most profound Bible students and saints"[1] that he had ever met.

Yet all we know of Lillian's early life and spiritual training is that she was raised as the daughter of a prominent Methodist minister. We also know that she was among the most educated of the women or men at Azusa Street, having attended Asbury College for a short period.

Lillian Anderson was the daughter of a Methodist minister and board member of Asbury College in Wilmore, Kentucky, a bastion of holiness thought. Alfred Garr was a young radical Holiness preacher. The couple met at the college and married the next year. They abruptly ended their studies two months later to go into full-time ministry.

Lillian and Alfred were ordained by both the Methodist church and the International Apostolic Prayer Union, a Holiness group led by famed evangelist Martin Wells Knapp. They shared the preaching platform with such notable Holiness speakers as Alma White of the Pillar of Fire and other Burning Bush regulars. By the time their journey together ended, they had visited such exotic locales as Hong Kong, India, China, Japan, and Ceylon. Lillian would emerge as a speaker in her own right and a "significant voice" in Pentecostal circles. After Lillian's death, Alfred would go on to pastor Stone Church in Charlotte, North Carolina, one of the largest Pentecostal churches on the East Coast at that time.

Initially, the Garrs started several congregations, but in each locale they left other people in place to pastor the churches. For a short time, Alfred served as pastor with the Burning Bush

Mission in Danville, Virginia. In February 1906, the Burning
Bush Organization appointed the couple to pastor their congregation in Los Angeles and to attempt to revive the troubled
church. Alfred was also appointed West Coast director of the
Burning Bush movement. Within a short period of time, the couple was able to begin to turn the congregation around.

Alfred and Lillian came to Azusa Street in early spring of 1906,
soon after the revival began. At first Alfred attended the meetings
alone, enthusiastically seeking the new experience. Lillian was initially skeptical of the new movement. Their intense disagreement
over the subject strained their relationship to the point that it
threatened to break up the marriage. But Alfred requested that
Lillian go to one meeting to judge its merits for herself.

She agreed to his request, and the two attended the service
together. On arriving, Lillian was immediately struck by the sin-
cerity of the people, felt what she saw, and experienced a move
of God. She shortly found herself praising God in tongues.
Though Alfred had been attending the services faithfully for a
short time, he had not received the Pentecostal baptism. Several
days later and after much soul-searching and repentance, Alfred
had the same experience.

There is some discrepancy about how the Garrs' congregation
reacted to the news of their Holy Spirit baptism. By one account,
when the Garrs went back to their Burning Bush congregation
and announced that they had received the Pentecostal experience
of tongues, they were immediately relieved of the pastorate. A
second account of the situation relates that not only did the
Garrs attend the Azusa Street meetings themselves, but at first
they temporarily closed their church so that members of the congregation could attend services with them. It also insists that
after a short time, Garr permanently closed his church and urged
members of the congregation to join with Seymour's meeting.

Some historians suggest that it was this move by Garr that
helped turn a revival populated by a small number of mostly
African American house servants into the large multiracial meet-

ing that the Azusa Street Revival became. By either account, the Garrs found themselves without a pastorate and eager to be involved again in ministry leadership. Certainly they, like so many other ministers at the Azusa Street Revival, were given an opportunity to testify and exhort as they felt directed by the Spirit, yet they held no official position at the Azusa Street Mission. It is not surprising then that, with no place to serve in leadership, they stayed at the revival for only a short while. Within a week of Alfred being baptized in the Holy Spirit, the couple announced to the congregation that they felt called as missionaries to India. Almost immediately, a man stood up and proclaimed that he would give five hundred dollars for the trip. A woman followed by giving two hundred dollars, and then another man gave one hundred. Within fifteen minutes, the congregation had raised an offering of several hundred dollars for their support. The couple saw this as God's confirmation of their call and began to prepare to leave.

In late June 1906, Alfred and Lillian left the mission to begin what was to become a spiritually fruitful, yet personally costly, missionary journey. From the beginning, their endeavor was to be a faith work, and the Garrs sought or accepted no regular support from any existing missionary organization.

First, the Garrs stopped in Chicago to meet with and receive a blessing from the officials of the Burning Bush Organization. From there, they went to Danville, Virginia, where Garr had formerly served as a pastor to hold revival meetings. Lillian and Alfred then went to New York from where they departed for the East. While in those cities, they continued to preach, share their testimonies, and spread the message of the Pentecostal blessing. Additionally, they held evangelistic campaigns that touched large crowds and won many converts from the Burning Bush Organization to the Pentecostal experience.

The Garrs regularly filed reports back to the Azusa Street Mission to be published in *The Apostolic Faith*. One article entitled "Good News from Danville, Virginia" summarized

their activities as they moved across the country on their way
to Asia:

> Brother and Sister A.G. Garr . . . were powerfully baptized with
> the Holy Ghost and received the gift of tongues, especially the
> language of India and dialects. Bro. Garr was able to pray a native
> of India "through" in his own language, the Bengali. Sister Garr
> also spoke Chinese. They left Los Angeles for the East in July
> going by the way of Chicago, where they met with the Burning
> Bush leaders, then on to Danville, Va., where they have been
> preaching to hungry souls. From there, they will go on to India.
>
> In a letter from Bro. Garr we learn that God is honoring His
> precious gospel in a marvelous way, reclaiming, sanctifying and
> filling with the Holy Ghost nearly all the members of the old
> Burning Bush band. The brother writes that when they spoke in
> tongues the people had such confidence in their Pentecostal bap-
> tism that those who were sick were immediately healed.[2]

In another, longer letter from the same city, titled "Pentecost
in Danville, Va.," the Garrs provided a more detailed description
of their preparation to leave and of their expectation of what
they would find on the mission field:

> Dear Saints in Los Angeles:
> We are making preparations to go to India as soon as possible.
> Three of us—with the baby, four in all—will go just as soon as
> possible, so as to be on the ocean in the right time.
>
> When we came here from Los Angeles, we found the band to
> whom we had preached while here before, most of them backslid-
> den and fussing among themselves. But when they saw that God
> had really done something wonderful for us, they all came in and
> began to seek the Lord. Most of them have been baptized with the
> Holy Ghost and have received the foreign tongue.
>
> One young girl received the baptism Friday night and she
> spoke in German. God sent us a German to interpret. He said he

could understand everything perfectly. Sister Jennie Eans has also received the German language, and speaks it very fluently.

. . . O, how I praise God that He ever gave us this wonderful experience of the baptism with the Holy Ghost. The folks fall under the power of God, and a great time is on here. The church was packed twice yesterday and altar overflowing with seekers. One saved man was sanctified in the afternoon meeting and in the evening meeting received the baptism with the Holy Ghost and spoke in tongues and magnified God.

A real revival has begun and three holiness preacher boys have fallen in line. Two of them have received the baptism and the tongues. The other one is seeking and says he will never stop till he receives it. A good many have received the tongues, we do not know how many[.]

The sick are being healed. Soon after we arrived, a lady sick with dropsy came to the meeting. She got out of bed to come; had been sick a long time. As she told us how glad she was to see us back in Danville and of her long sick spell, I said: "God will heal you," and took her hand. She immediately shouted that she was healed. I felt the healing power flow into her body. The next day she told us that her limbs were swollen, but that every bit of it was driven out at once. She walked down town and then told her neighbors about the wonderful things the Lord had done for her. Several have been healed. But, best of all, many are getting the light, and as the Bible opens to us, they rejoice for the precious truths that have been hidden from us for so long by the "traditions of the elders." This is the greatest power I ever saw. Glory to God! I have wanted just this for years, but did not know how to get it. But, Hallelujah! . . . .

We are expecting God to give us a good revival in India. Pray for us.[3]

Initially, Alfred and Lillian firmly believed that God had given them the gift of xenolalia—the ability to speak in a known tongue that is not one's own—with the baptism of the Holy

Spirit. Alfred believed that he had received the Bengali language, one of the several dialects of India, and reported that while they were still in Los Angeles, he was able to "pray a native Indian through in his own language."[4] Lillian believed that she was given Tibetan and Mandarin, and while still in Danville, the Garrs reported that "she improves everyday in Tibetan and Chinese."[5] They believed that they would have the use of this supernatural ability on the mission field without having to learn languages. When their efforts to utilize tongues in evangelism and preaching failed, A. G. abandoned his insistence that tongues were a missionary tool. Lillian then began to study the Chinese language, devoting several hours a day to learning its grammatical rules, nuances, syntax, and pronunciation.[6]

For six years after leaving the Azusa Street Revival, the Garrs traveled throughout the United States, Hong Kong, India, and China preaching the Pentecostal message. From the outset, they worked as a ministry team with both of them ministering in the services they conducted. Lillian's anointed preaching and teaching made her participation in these meetings as sought after as that of her husband's. Reports filed back to the mission and to other organs generally carried both their names. And both suffered a great deal for the sake of the gospel.

The Garrs, accompanied by their two-year-old daughter and her nurse, Maria Gardner, arrived in Hong Kong for the first time in October 1906, where they stayed for several months. Lillian was pregnant with their second child. In October 1909, upon returning to Hong Kong, Lillian was pregnant again and their son, Alfred, Jr., was born in April of the next year. While A. G. was involved in outreach to the non-Christians, Lillian spent her time teaching members of the mission church. During this tenure, the Garrs opened a home to disciple and support other missionaries who came to the field.

The Garrs arrived in Calcutta, India, for the first time in Spring 1907 to visit and minister at a conference of missionaries.

LILLIAN ANDERSON GARR | 93

Again they wrote back to Azusa Street about their work. Their correspondence appeared in an article in *The Apostolic Faith* entitled "The Work in India" in June of that year:

". . . Some of the choicest spirits of India have been baptized with the Holy Ghost. It is wonderful to hear one of these tell how for nine years she had hunted meetings where she could receive the Holy Ghost, and how she has found Him whom her soul so long has craved. She and her friend are missionaries from Columbo, Ceylon. One of them has been clearly healed of a disease of several years standing. . . .

A prominent missionary who has been baptized with the Holy Ghost and has received wonderful power has thrown open the doors of her beautiful mission home and today is preaching the word with power. . . .

The Lord also gave Sister Garr a vision of Himself one night, while in Calcutta and His hands were filled with golden crowns ready to place on heads. And the same evening, He gave her the message "Let no man take thy crown." A missionary arose and said that on that day God had spoken those words to her, and she did not know what it meant. . . .

In a school of 1,500 native girls and 200 boys . . . the head of the school has been tarrying and the Comforter has come to her and also to her daughter, a number of her teachers, and 300 native girls. Hallelujah! At Dhond, a school of boys, numbers have been saved, some are speaking in tongues.

In Calcutta, one Missionary who was baptized in the meeting went back to her high school and in a short time forty-five precious native girls were baptized in the Spirit. Then the matron of a Rescue Home received her Pentecost and shortly the dear girls who had been redeemed from such lives of sin, were learning how to glorify Jesus and the Holy Ghost was given. . . .

False reports have been circulated of the work in India. Do not believe them. Bro. and Sister A. G. Garr[7]

The couple arrived back in India in February 1910 where they worked among English and native communities, holding meetings through central and northern regions of the country over a four-month period. In August 1911, they again returned to China, where they stayed for eight months and hosted a rest home for other missionaries, having up to forty in the residence at one time.

During their several trips to Hong Kong, Lillian took on an entirely new venture when she became greatly concerned for the physical as well as spiritual well-being of Chinese women. She wanted to help ensure their eternal salvation as well as improve their temporal existence. One area of particular concern for her was the practice of binding the feet of young Chinese girls in order to keep them small, an attribute considered beautiful by Chinese tradition.

Lillian saw the crippling effects of this practice, and since Hong Kong was a British colony, began to challenge both the Chinese people and the British government over it. At a time when women were still emerging as spokespersons for social issues in Western society, Lillian's efforts on behalf of Chinese women were considered extraordinary. The British consulate instructed her that they had no intention of taking the Chinese to task over this matter. But Garr wouldn't relent and committed herself to seeing the practice outlawed.

She began attacking the practice on biblical terms and slowly began to see a change in heart within the Chinese people she touched. Her efforts also eventually brought about a change of mind in the British government, and they outlawed anyone coming from the mainland of China and settling in Hong Kong to practice this custom. When the women of Hong Kong saw the great length of her efforts of their behalf, many of them converted to Christianity.

For a short while when they returned to the U.S. in 1912, Alfred pastored a small congregation in Los Angeles even though they spent the next five years traveling throughout the United

States and Canada holding evangelistic and faith-healing campaigns. During this time, Alfred returned to the East, going to India, Arabia, and China, while Lillian stayed home with their young son. In 1914, the Garrs settled down from their travels and planted a new congregation in Los Angeles.

Despite such great victories, the Garrs paid a heavy personal price for their work on the mission field. Not only did they experience deprivation and the necessity to depend on God for their daily sustenance, but there were times when that sustenance was meager at best. But they were to pay an even harsher price with the loss of two of their children. Though they had prayed and believed God for healing hundreds of others, physical healing did not manifest itself in their own circumstances. During their first tour of duty in Hong Kong in 1907, Lillian was pregnant with their second daughter who was delivered stillborn. The first daughter, Virginia, succumbed to smallpox fever at the age of two. Their son was born prematurely, weighing only three pounds, and was only given a slight chance to live because initially he could not keep milk in his stomach. But reportedly, A. G. had a vision in which the Lord instructed him to find and give the child condensed milk, a product that was rarely heard of and scarcely available in the area where they were stationed. It was only after the Garrs located a source for the milk and began to feed it to the boy that his situation turned around and he was able to gain strength. As an adult, Alfred Jr. helped his father in ministry.

Like many others, Lillian Garr shared her dramatic testimony with *The Apostolic Faith* readership. It was written from Colombo, Ceylon:

When the Comforter first came my heart was so overflowing with the joy, I had not time to prove the blessed reality of the experience received in dear old Azusa Street Mission? but as persecution arose in India I have proved day by day, hour by hour that He abides and reveals Jesus to my soul in wonderful ways.

How conscious have I been of His presence giving "songs of deliverance" and speaking through me to my own comfort and delight. Praise Him. There are several hundred natives baptized with the Holy Ghost and speaking in tongues today in India. I want to add, that the blessed Comforter does indeed reveal the perfect life of the Savior, not alone in the oil of joy, ("Thou hast loved righteousness and hated iniquity; therefore God even Thy God, hath anointed Thee with the oil of gladness above Thy fellows"), but the other side of this precious life, ("The man of sorrows and acquainted with grief.") And we can say we have not longed for the joy side alone, but to "suffer with Him that we might reign with Him." He longs for a bride who shares both His suffering and joy. I want to enter into His own heart and feel as He felt, letting His joy be my joy, His sorrow my sorrow. He has put groanings into my heart which cannot be uttered over a lost world and those who do not understand His workings in the earth at this time. How I praise Him for a love for my enemies that is not natural but divine. Hallelujah.

We long to see all power restored that the heathen can no more say to the missionaries: "Where is their God?" Joel 2:17. "The Lord will be jealous for His land and pity His people."

Our hearts are knit with the dear Saints at Azusa Street and we think with love of all. How often I think of the times the Spirit sang through Sister Crawford and me: "Jesus, Savior, pilot me, over life's tempestuous sea."

That testified to my own heart that much would arise for which the Spirit was preparing me. He abides, the blessed Comforter.

—Mrs. Lillian Garr[8]

Lillian's missionary trips which twice took her nearly three-quarters around the world, brought her both the intense joy of seeing hundreds saved and many having their own Pentecostal experience as well as the overwhelming sorrow in losing two children and a trusted companion to disease. In 1916, Lillian Garr died in Los Angeles at the age of thirty-eight. She had been seriously ill for some time with an undisclosed illness. Despite the prayers of the saints on several continents, she showed no signs of improvement. Alfred was counseled by doctors that the only hope was surgery. He agreed to the operation, but Lillian died of complications from the procedure.

Her stature in the Pentecostal movement was expressed by the fact that more than twelve hundred people representing the leaders and rank and file from every segment of the Holiness-Pentecostal movement attended her funeral. This was especially exceptional since, by then, the movement had begun to splinter into the various schismatic factions that were to plague it for the rest of its existence. On this rare occasion, people from oneness groups, finished work groups, and the Holiness-Pentecostal groups bridged their schisms and gathered to pay homage to an individual. Lillian Garr was a rare person who was esteemed by members of these various factions. Alfred remarked at her funeral that in their "various travels together, people had different opinions" concerning him, "but everybody loved her."[9] This sums up the esteem in which she was held by Holiness and Pentecostal leaders and rank and file adherents.

In an article commemorating her death that appeared in the May 1916 issue of *Confidence,* Stanley Frodsham, an early Assemblies of God official and Pentecostal historian, indicates her significance for her place in the Pentecostal movement.

> It would be difficult to find one more universally loved in Pentecostal circles and I believe I speak for all who have ever heard her when I write that we have lost the most spiritual teacher we had from our ranks . . . . She always had something fresh from God. She was a woman of abundant revelations and always gave forth her message under a mighty annointing of the Spirit. With her husband, she has preached the Pentecostal message around the globe.[10]

Their assertion points to the high esteem in which she was held by Holiness and Pentecostal leaders and rank and file adherents.

chapter 9

Susie Villa Valdez

MOST OF THE LATINOS WHO CAME TO Azusa Street were Roman Catholics. Many of them were adherents of the Franciscan branch of Catholicism with its heritage of openness to spiritual gifts, including speaking in tongues and divine healing. So they were open to the phenomena that they encountered at the revival and did not find many of them unusual at all. Among those sharing this heritage was Mexican American Susie Villa Valdez, a seamstress by profession and a devout member of this branch of Catholicism, who had been saved under the ministry of Finis Yoakum, a medical doctor turned evangelist and faith healer.

Although open to the spiritual gifts as shared in Catholicism, Susie experienced a degree of discomfort to the spiritual climate of the Pentecostal outpouring at Azusa Street, and her earliest encounters with the revival were unsettling. Like many others who visited the services, her first personal experience of the power of the Holy Spirit was not speaking in tongues, but rather a sense of dissatisfaction with her own spiritual condition that took a physical, mental, and emotional toll on her. As her son, A. C. Valdez, later recounts:

> My mother thought that something was wrong with her—perhaps heart trouble. She went from doctor to doctor. All of them said the same thing, "Mrs. Valdez, you have a strong heart. There

is nothing wrong with you." . . . No human physician could help her, so she went to the greatest physician. Kneeling in her room, she prayed, "Lord, if I have no heart problem, give me what I need."

From that moment on, she had the witness of the Spirit that she was saved—she was born again. Soon after that she received the baptism of the Holy Ghost with fire at Azusa Street.[1]

We know about Susie Valdez primarily through the writings of A. C. who, as a young man, attended the meetings with his mother and later became a prominent evangelist in the Pentecostal movement and the Assemblies of God.

The Valdez family attended the Azusa Street meetings from very early in the revival and belonged to the mission congregation until 1909. During this time, Seymour had a break with the Latino members of his congregation that resulted in most of them leaving. Susie's activities at the Azusa Street meetings, however, go unreported. Although the multiracial climate of the mission at first invited full participation and input from people of all nationalities, Susie did not contribute to *The Apostolic Faith* newspaper or hold any official position in the mission. But she attended the meetings faithfully between 1906 and 1909, often in the company of her husband and young son. Susie was probably among the Latinos who exuberantly worshiped and gave their testimonies. Through her testimony and ministry outside the revival services, she led many other Latino seekers through the mission.

Before arriving at Azusa Street, Susie had worked alongside Dr. Yoakum at Pisgah House in Arroyo Seco. Though a medical doctor, Yoakum suffered from a debilitating injury for which medical science could offer no cure. After seeking and receiving divine healing in 1895, he gave up his formal medical practice to establish Pisgah House as a mission for the needy. This ministry offered housing, medical care, food and clothing, along with spiritual support to the homeless, alcoholics, drug addicts, prostitutes, and those who were simply indigent. By 1911, the home and a number of sister locations provided housing for 173 people, 9,000 clean beds, and 18,000 meals monthly in the Los Angeles area.

Since the home was a faith ministry, it was supported solely by contributions and staffed primarily by volunteers. Susie Valdez could be counted among this number and regularly assisted with the Spanish-speaking individuals who came seeking a variety of services. After her Azusa Street encounter, she continued her involvement here but broadened her ministry by moving out to the city slums where she played her guitar, sang, and preached. She also went to the migrant labor camps of Redlands, Riverside, and San Bernardino, some sixty miles east of Los Angeles, to witness to the hundreds of Latinos swarming into these areas to fill the demand for cheap labor. Her witness among the Spanish community was instrumental in drawing many of them to the Azusa Street meetings.

> The mother of A. C. Valdez, Sr . . . went from Azusa Street to Riverside to hold a Sunday afternoon meeting among the Spanish people. Many English-speaking people attended. Among these was the owner of a large orange orchard, a brother of Norman Chandler, president and co-owner of the Los Angeles Times. He received a marvelous baptism of the Holy Ghost. After this, many of the Spanish people from far and near went to Azusa Street.[2]

Among her audience were the same prostitutes, alcoholics, and derelicts who were served by Pisgah House but had returned to their regular lives on the street. Susie would play her guitar and sing as they gathered on the street corner, waiting attentively as she would tell of the miraculous, life-changing occurrences that were regularly unfolding at the Azusa Street Revival.

Along with her public ministry, Susie regularly prayed for the salvation of her family—her husband José de Jesús Valdez and her two sons. Despite being a devout Catholic, José was a chain-smoker, and Susie was unsure of his salvation. He had been an invalid for some time. When Susie first learned of the miracles happening at Yoakum's faith-healing home, she urged her husband to attend meetings there. Although he may have accompanied her, there was no evidence of divine healing.

Susie prayed earnestly for her husband's salvation and coaxed him to faithfully attend the Azusa Street meetings. He finally agreed and was baptized with the Holy Spirit at the revival, after which he experienced his own miraculous healing. In his case, however, the healing was not instantaneous. José experienced a gradual improvement that culminated with the disappearance of a large growth from his body.

Susie also took her family to the 1913 Arroyo Seco camp meeting conducted by R. J. Scott. Scott was a Christian businessman associated with the Azusa Street Mission. This meeting became a significant gathering in the early years of the Pentecostal revival. There Susie and her family were able to hear renowned preachers and faith healers such as Maria Woodworth-Etter and Carrie Judd Montgomery, who had both embraced the Pentecostal faith. A. C. Valdez, Sr., was a teenager at the time of the Arroyo Seco meeting, but it was to have a profound impact on his life.[3]

Though Susie's ministry broadened to include evangelistic speaking among some of the small Latino congregations that formed in and around Los Angeles, her major impact was on the life and ministry of at least one early Pentecostal leader. Her son A. C. was little more than a young spectator when his mother first took him to the Azusa Street meetings. The ten-year-old boy did not understand all that was going on but recounts that Susie simply explained, "The power of the Holy Ghost has fallen. This is like what happened at Pentecost in the New Testament of the Bible."[4] It would be several months before he had his own Pentecostal Spirit baptism, spurred by an experience during which Susie approached his bed late one night while he was sleeping.

My mother came into my dark bedroom after a service at the Azusa Street Mission. She bent over and touched my shoulder . . . and began talking fast in some language I had never heard before. . . . Then she began crying, but I knew right away she was crying for joy, not sadness. . . . Then the other language stopped and she said: "Son, I have just had the most glorious experience. I have just been baptized in the Holy Ghost and have been given the gift of tongues". . . .

Now I was eager to see what was going on at Azusa Street! On the next night she invited me along. As when I came within a block of the two-story, white painted building, I felt a "pulling sensation." I couldn't have turned away if I wanted to.[5]

It was not until several years later, after a period of backsliding, that he finally accepted the Christian faith and embraced Holy Spirit baptism. A. C. was to become one of the foremost evangelists of his day in the Assembly of God. His ministry was not restricted to the Latino community, as he spread the gospel around the world.

On occasion, Susie traveled with her son to revival meetings in the United States and around the world. Within these meetings, she provided prayer support, sang, and gave her testimony of the miraculous experience of Azusa Street as well as of her own life and ministry. In her later years and after the death of her husband, she lived with her son and his family.

During her lifetime, Susie remained a spiritual influence in her son's life. A. C. regarded her counsel seriously and sometimes used her as a gauge for the direction of his ministry. One incident in the later years of her life is exemplary: A. C. was praying during a time of particularly deep discouragement in his life and felt God giving him a specific message—one that he did not completely understand. Susie was in another room of the house praying when the same message came to her mind. A. C. tells it this way:

Alone in my room, near the closed door, I knelt and prayed. . . .
I did not know that mother was in the next room . . . [and] had
also knelt and prayed. . . . Then the Lord spoke clearly to me. "Go
to Sunshine! Go to Sunshine!" Sunshine? Did He want me to go
out into the sunshine or was there a place called that? I just had
to tell the Lord's message to the others. My mother already had a
hold of the doorknob on the other side. I almost pulled her on top
of me. "I know what we're supposed to do," she cried exultant-
ly. "The Lord just spoke to me. . . . Arise, and go to Sunshine."

A. C. saw this as a miraculous confirmation from God. He
later learned that Sunshine was a suburb of Melbourne,
Australia. The entire family—A. C., his wife, children, and mother—proceeded to make plans to go to Sunshine. The meeting at
Sunshine was the beginning of what A. C. was to characterize as
a "great revival" throughout Australia that lasted an entire year.[6]
Susie Valdez evangelized until she was almost ninety years old.
During this period, she continued to travel by train or bus across
the United States, playing the guitar, singing, and preaching the
gospel wherever she was invited. She died shortly after retiring
from ministry.

chapter 10

Rosa de Lopez

T HE SECOND EDITION OF *The Apostolic Faith* newspaper, published in October 1906 (eight months after the revival began), reported that there were "a good many Spanish speaking people in Los Angeles."[1] It was referring to the several thousand Hispanic Americans and new immigrants among the Los Angeles population of nearly 300,000. Most of the Spanish community was Catholic, and the majority of individuals were from Mexico. Many had come to escape from the war in their country, and many more came to pursue the promise of a better life in the land of plenty.

From the very beginning, Latinos flocked to the Azusa Street Mission in search of a transcendent God. They were drawn by the reports in the secular press and throughout the Christian community of the miraculous and supernatural signs and wonders that made the revival at Azusa Street a "veritable Mecca to which came pilgrims from all over the world."[2]

Rosa and Abundio de Lopez were Mexican immigrants who had migrated to California and settled in the San Diego area in 1902, which was also the year they married. The Lopez family shared many firsts among the Latinos that came to the revival. They arrived at the mission in May 1906, a little more than one month after the revival moved to its new quarters. Possibly among the first Latinos to visit the mission, they were among the first Latinos to be baptized with "Holy Ghost and fire." Whether they had been in the ministry before coming to Azusa Street is unknown. Less than one month later, when they received their Pentecostal experience, they were the first Spanish-speaking Pentecostal evangelists in North America. "Thanks be to God for the Spirit which brought us to the Azusa Street Mission, the Apostolic Faith, old-time religion," they exclaimed. "We cannot express our gratitude and thanksgiving which we feel moment by moment for what He has done for us, so we want to be used for the healing of both soul and body."[3]

The multicultural atmosphere made it extremely comfortable for all races and ethnic groups to feel at home in the revival. As one lay Methodist participant asserted, the revival "did not start in any church in this city, but out in the barn, so that we might all come and take part in it. If it had started in a fine church, poor colored people and Spanish people would not have got in, but praise God it started here."[4] Within this setting, it did not matter whether one spoke English. People would speak in their own languages, and the expression on their faces and their exuberant body language would convey a message of holy excitement about what God was doing in their lives.

The Lopez family remained at the Azusa Street Mission for at least three years. They were both evangelists, and Rosa served diligently beside her husband. Abundio worked as a manual laborer by day. In the evenings, they worked at the altar together, praying with sinners for conversion and for the converted to be sanctified or receive the baptism of the Holy Spirit. They evangelized the Mexican population of Los Angeles by holding street meetings in the nearby Mexican open-air plaza. By December they traveled together to evangelize in their hometown of San Diego, 120 miles south of Los Angeles. After a short stay, they returned to Los Angeles, where they continued to evangelize among the Latino community. A report of their efforts appeared in an article entitled "Preaching to The Spanish," published in the November 1906 volume of *The Apostolic Faith*: "Brother and Sister Lopez, Spanish people, who are filled with the Holy Spirit, are being used of God in street meetings and in helping Mexicans at the altar at Azusa Street."[5]

In 1909, William Seymour rewarded Abundio for his faithfulness to the mission by ordaining him to ministry. There is no record of Rosa being ordained, though she had been active with her husband in ministry from the beginning.

The two probably joined the other Latinos who left the mission later that year. For reasons that are not entirely clear, their unbridled enthusiasm and zealousness to testify about what God was accomplishing in their lives and ministries apparently prompted the leader of the mission to "ruthlessly crush" the Latino contingent.[6] Their exodus along with a decline in white attendance signaled the end of the multiracial climate of the congregation. From that point on it was primarily an African American mission whose attendance continued to steadily decline.

Rosa's and Abundio's testimony appears in the October 1906 edition of the newspaper. Because they were anxious to reach Latinos in their own language, it was first printed in Spanish with the following English translation:

> We testify to the power of the Holy Spirit in forgiveness, sanctification, and the baptism with the Holy Ghost and fire. We give thanks to God for this wonderful gift which we have received from Him, according to the promise. Thanks be to God for the Spirit which brought us to the Azusa Street Mission, the Apostolic Faith, old-time religion, I and my wife, on the 29th of last May. I came for sanctification, and thank God also for the baptism with the Holy Ghost and fire which I received on the 5th of June, 1905. We cannot express the gratitude and thanksgiving which we feel moment by moment for what He has done for us, so we want to be used for the salvation and healing of both soul and body. I am a witness of His wonderful promise and marvelous miracles by the Holy Ghost, by faith in the Lord Jesus Christ. May God bless you all.[7]

In 1908, Rosa developed a "stone" tumor, which worsened by 1911 to the point that it caused constant vomiting. Abundio and others did not expect her to live. But being believers in divine healing, he did not want to subject her to surgery. By 1915, while serving as a pastor in Los Angeles, Abundio was desperately seeking help for his wife and decided to take her to Finis Yoakum's faith healing-home. Shortly afterward, he felt led to carry her to one of famed faith healer Maria Woodworth-Etter's meetings. Woodworth-Etter prayed with Rosa, who was healed of the tumor.

Brother Lopez brought his wife to the meeting Saturday, October 9, and Sister Etter prayed for her at 8:30 P.M. and when she commanded the devil to loosen his hold on her and said, "I take the sword of the Spirit and cut this evil tumor out loose in the name of the Lord!" The tumor was immediately cut loose as if a surgeon's knife had been used and both were filled with the power and went home and waited on God for full evidence. And at 3:30 A.M. Sunday, the stone tumor passed away, root and branch. Glory to God! She didn't have to stay in bed to convalesce, as she would have done had a surgeon performed the operation. We have a wonderful Physician.[8]

Neither Rosa nor Abundio were educated people, as even the Spanish version of their testimony showed poor grammar. Presumably then, their English skills were worse. It did not matter, however, for neither language nor grammar was considered a barrier to communicating within the revival: "If a Mexican or German cannot speak English, he gets up and speaks in his own tongue and feels quite at home for the Spirit interprets through the face and the people say 'Amen.'"[9]

Within several years of the beginning of the Azusa Street revivals, there were a number of Mexican congregations throughout California. While Abundio continued to serve as pastor of a congregation in Los Angeles, additional congregations sprang up under other leaders in other sections of Los Angeles and in San Diego. Additionally, others opened in Riverside, San

Bernardino, and Colton. The efforts of Rosa and Abundio Lopez and many others have resulted in the more than one million Latino Pentecostals who are currently in more than ten thousand congregations throughout the United States.

chapter 11

Ardella Knapp Mead

B Y THE TIME SHE AND IIER HUSBAND arrived at the Azusa Street Revival, Ardella Knapp Mead was sixty-three years old, making her the oldest of the women leaders who emerged from the revival. She was also among the most seasoned woman ministers, since for twenty years she and her husband Samuel had been Methodist Episcopal Church missionaries in Africa. Both were well-known within Holiness mission circles, having worked for more than fourteen years in Malange, Angola, as part of frontier pastor and missionary, William Taylor's original famous "pioneer forty."

In 1885, Taylor arrived in Angola with a team that helped him set up the first Methodist missions effort in Africa. He eventually organized and operated a string of mission stations throughout the Luanda and Malange regions. But according to Taylor, the Meads made the Malange station one of his most prosperous, and he was to later admiringly write of them in his memoirs: "If there were one thousand trainers such as Samuel Mead and Ardella, his wife, there would in a few years be twenty thousand native pastors and evangelists in Africa under the leadership of our all conquering King."[1]

Before going to Africa, "Ardie" (as she was called by her husband) and Samuel had been farmers in Vermont. This experience served them well, since as part of Taylor's group, the Meads were required to earn their own support for traveling to the mission field. They were required to maintain their own sustenance without accepting support from any individuals or missions organizations at home.

From the outset, the goal of Taylor's missions was to convert as many as possible and to train the African converts to take over the leadership of the newly established churches, schools, and other facilities. As part of their efforts to reach this goal, the Meads not only taught Bible study and preached gospel messages in the worship services but also taught reading, agriculture, and other skills required to equip their converts to be self-sufficient. Ardella was a musician and music teacher who employed this skill to train musicians for the newly established churches. They had no children of their own but adopted several African children, whom they raised to adulthood. When they returned to America, their "children," many of them grown by that time, remained in Africa.

In 1896, the work of Taylor's group was taken over by the Missionary Society of the Methodist Episcopal Church. By 1906, Taylor had died, and the Meads returned to America on furlough for a vitally needed rest and spiritual rejuvenation. In an article entitled "Sister Mead's Baptism," published in the November 1906 edition of *The Apostolic Faith,* Ardella recalls the circumstances that led them first to Los Angeles, then to the Azusa Street Revival:

Two years before we left Africa, the Holy Spirit began to speak to us in a special way. We felt the lack of the power and love in the service of our Master, and we commenced seeking that power from Him; we had no definite light on the baptism in our sanctified life of twenty years. And praise God, we did have a most wonderful experience when we were justified, and our sins forgiven. And then after we were sanctified, the joy of heaven filled our souls, and we had the wonderful "anointing which abideth." Yet we felt the lack of power in our lives, and this was what we were earnestly seeking, as we waited on God in our little mission home in Africa.

Just before our return to America, we believe it was the Spirit of God, who said to us very plainly, "Los Angeles, California, is the end of your journey." This seemed strange to us, at the time, as we had no friends in Los Angeles; but we see now it was the Holy Spirit of God, to bring us to Los Angeles to receive our Pentecost. . . .

About this time, we met a sister in Christ, who told us of the Azusa Street meetings, and that some were speaking in tongues, so we went at once to see if these things were true.[2]

Shortly after arriving in Los Angeles, Ardella was stricken with pneumonia in both lungs and became gravely ill. However, she soon recovered. Whether that healing occurred at Azusa Street was not noted. The Meads came to the Azusa Street meetings sometime between late July and early September 1906. They looked for and fully embraced the spiritual fervency they found there. In Ardella's words, "I went to the meetings when I first heard of the manifestation of the Spirit, speaking in tongues, healing of the body, etc. I was not surprised, for we had been praying and expecting something of this kind to arouse God's people to the reality of the Word of God, and the truth of God Emanuel."[3]

Although the Meads were hungry for spiritual empowerment, the Holy Spirit baptism did not come easy to Ardella, who recounted her prolonged struggle to receive the experience in an article in *The Apostolic Faith:*

We felt the power of God immediately as we entered the meeting. After two or three days, as the invitation was given for those who wished to seek for the baptism of the Holy Ghost, I went forward to the little humble altar. While on the way the enemy said to me, "You, a missionary in Africa twenty years, now going forward to the altar." I said, yes, I am going forward, for I want all that God has for me, and then and there I gained a real victory in my soul. Then Bro. Seymour, Sister Crawford, and another Sister laid their hands upon me that I might receive the Holy Ghost. As they prayed, I felt the power go through my body, but did not receive then the full baptism.

We waited on God daily in our home for three weeks, searching the Scriptures, confessing our faults, and getting everything under the blood, even forgetting at times to take food. During this time, while attending the meetings one day, the tongues became a stone of stumbling to me, and a rock of offense, and I immediately went into darkness, which was so great that my dear husband cried to the Lord for me, and I was restored, willing to submit what I did not understand to God. Then the enemy tried to get me discouraged, telling me that this baptism was not for me. I went into my room feeling so discouraged, when the Spirit said to me as plainly as a voice, "How did you receive your justification? How did you receive your sanctification?" I said, Lord, by faith. He then said, "Receive me." I arose, and felt very happy, praising the Lord. This was on Friday evening and we went into our front room and said we would have a meeting to seek the Spirit just as they did at Bro. Seymour's. So we sang and testified, and then fell on our knees in prayer. As we repeated over and over again, we receive the Holy Ghost, in our simplicity, he came in, and we could not retire until late. Then we asked the Holy Spirit to continue His work in us while we slept.

On Saturday morning at the breakfast table I said, something seems to hinder my perfect freedom, and my husband said, "It may be in regard to your little neighbor; you know she did not receive the gospel, and left off coming in to see you, and so you have left off going in to see her. You have more light than she, and perhaps have done wrong." The faithful Holy Spirit convicted me, and I said, beginning to cry like a child, Oh, Lord, I see it and fell on my knees. Just as I did this crying "let it all be under the blood," the Holy Ghost fell upon me in great sweetness and power; and just then I had a wonderful revelation of the blood of Christ making me as clean and innocent as a child, and Jesus was real to me.

—Ardell[a] K. Mead.[4]

When Ardella received the Holy Spirit baptism with tongues, she reportedly received an African dialect. She also had the ability to understand and corroborate messages given by others in African dialect. Armed with this tool, the Meads were the first persons at the revival to identify the tongues spoken by participants as genuine modern languages. How much of this ability was due to the gift of interpretation of tongues or to the twenty years of hearing such dialects on the mission field is unknown. A short piece in *The Apostolic Faith* describes her facility with languages in this way:

A young sister . . . speaks and sings in tongues as the Spirit gives utterance. She also interprets, and the following interpretation was also corroborated by Sister S. K. Mead, twenty years a missionary in Africa. Sister Mead arose and said that the language spoken was their dialect in Africa, a beautiful language, but one that is very difficult for English-speaking people to acquire, but the Holy Ghost, through the young lady, had given the perfect accent.[5]

Ironically, the Meads were among the few Azusa Street adherents who experienced the gift of xenolalia without tying it specifically to the ability to preach in the vernacular of the countries in which they were called to minister. Indeed, Samuel contended that when [m]any ask, "Do you think these tongues will be used in a foreign field?" he would simply answer, "As for myself I cannot say, My God is able, this I know."[6]

The Meads' former experience as missionaries proved to be an asset to the Azusa Street Mission in a number of ways. First, as noted, they were able to identify various African dialects that were spoken in tongues. Secondly, they were able to provide information about Africa to those who had never been there but felt newly called to the continent. And lastly, they knew the reality of conditions in Africa and could help prepare their spiritually ready comrades for the practical realities of life on the mission field.

From the time they first arrived at the Azusa Street Revival, the Meads expected to return to Africa as missionaries. By November 1906, they left Azusa Street in a group of seven, including Robert and Myrtle Shideler, Daisy and G.W. Batman, and Samuel's niece Bertha. They were part of the larger group of individuals of whom, as reported in *The Apostolic Faith,* God was using to "solve the missionary problem by sending out new-tongued missionaries on the apostolic faith line, without purse or scrip, and the Lord is going before them preparing the way."[7]

On the way to Africa, they first stopped in New York, where the Meads and the Batmans ministered together in preaching their new Pentecostal faith. The entire group shared testimonies of their own experience of Holy Spirit baptism. Without delineating each person's role, Samuel was simply to report that "Pentecost has surely fallen in New York in a mission there. A number have been baptized with the Holy Ghost and are speaking in new tongues."[8] It was here that the Meads and Batmans encountered and ministered to Thomas Barratt, the Holiness leader who was to become the leader of the Pentecostal movement in Norway. They then went on to Liverpool, England, where they worked among African immigrants. There the group split, and the Batmans joined Julia Hutchins and Lucy Farrow to sail for Liberia.

The Meads arrived in Benguela, a port city in western Angola, in January 1907. They were accompanied by Samuel's niece Bertha, who was a translator, teacher, and preacher. Robert and Myrtle Shideler, whom the Meads saw as an answer to their prayer for God to send "a young couple to take back with them to the work,"[9] were also with them. While at their post, Bertha contracted an unknown disease and died. Once in Africa, the group did not send any recorded reports back to *The Apostolic Faith*.

In October 1908, two years after they left Azusa Street, the Meads were back in Vermont caring for two of their invalid sisters and longing to return to Los Angeles. By the next year, they had retired from the mission field and settled in Los Angeles. Ardella Mead died in 1934 at the age of ninety-one.

chapter 12

Daisy Batman

A MONG THE WOMEN AND MEN who left the Azusa Street
Revival to carry the message of Pentecostal Spirit baptism
around the world, none was to pay a greater personal toll
than Daisy Batman and her husband, G. W. With very little
information on Daisy's background, except that she was saved as
a young teenager and experienced sanctification a year before
coming to Azusa Street, we pick up her story from a few short
articles about her and her husband in three issues of *The
Apostolic Faith* newsletter. Indeed, most of the information
comes from the December 1906 issue.

Daisy and G. W. came to Azusa Street and received their
Pentecostal experience in the early months of the revival. A short
item in the October 1906 issue of *The Apostolic Faith* simply
states that "Bro G. W. Batman and wife, Daisy, are saved, sanctified and baptized with the Holy Ghost and were given the
xenolalic gift of languages."[1] G. W. claimed that through this gift
he was able to speak six distinct languages.[2]

Three years before coming to Azusa Street, G. W. felt called
by God to go to Africa as a missionary. As part of that call, he
experienced a vision of a town on the west coast of the continent
and felt the Lord specifically leading him to that location. Later
at the revival, when he relayed this vision to Samuel Mead, Mead
responded that it was the perfect description of Monrovia,
Liberia. At first, Daisy felt the call to missions was specifically

for her husband and initially was willing to let him go while she stayed behind and cared for their three small children. After seeking more clarity from God, however, Daisy was convinced that the call to the mission field was for both of them. She determined then that they would go as a family. This decision was later to prove ominous for the entire family.

The Batmans were at Azusa Street for only a few months and had departed by December 1906. It is not reported what role they played in the revival. While there, however, they became acquainted with several single missionaries and missionary couples that shared their passion for and call to take the Pentecostal message to Africa. Many among this group shared the belief that they had been especially equipped by the Spirit with the gift of xenolalia, supernaturally equipping them with the ability to speak the African languages necessary to carry out ministry on the continent.

Three months after receiving the Pentecostal experience of Holy Spirit baptism, the Batmans left Los Angeles with two other missionary couples, Ardella and Samuel Mead and Robert and Myrtle Shideler. The team traveled together as far as Liverpool, England. There they split up. The Batmans went on to Liberia with Lucy Farrow and Julia Hutchins, while the Meads and Shidelers went further south to Benguela, Angola.

It was customary for many embarking from Azusa Street to stop in several cities in the U.S. on the way to their intended destination. Wherever the train stopped for a layover, they stayed from several hours to several days and engaged in ministry to whatever audience they could gather. Often there was only enough time to hold a makeshift meeting at the train platform. Other times they held street meetings or protracted tent revivals. Sometimes they were invited to speak to existing congregations about the revival back West. Many preached fiery sermons, but they also shared their personal testimonies of the Pentecostal experience. Sometimes these host congregations had already received word of the explosive happenings in Los Angeles either through reports from *The Apostolic Faith* or letters from friends or family who had been there. Often they were waiting anxiously for a face-to-face encounter with someone who had actually participated in the services.

So when the Batmans stopped in Topeka, Kansas, in December 1906, the congregation of Holiness believers warmly and enthusiastically welcomed them. They listened intently as Daisy shared her testimony about the Azusa Street Revival and G. W. preached sermons regarding the Holy Spirit baptism with tongues.

In New York, Steven Merritt, pastor of a "large tabernacle," gave Bro. Batman the opportunity to address his congregation. This opportunity was to prove to have far-reaching consequences for the new movement. Among those in attendance was Thomas Ball Barratt, a Norwegian Holiness pastor and leader in the international Holiness movement. He was deeply moved by Batman's preaching and later in the service asked Lucy Leatherman (another Azusa Street woman who was attending the meeting) to pray with him to receive the Pentecostal experience of tongues. Barratt then went on to carry the Pentecostal message to Norway and several other European countries, including Sweden, Finland, Germany, and Russia.

With three small children and no finances to support their trip, Daisy and G. W. were willing to "trust the Lord" for their fare and sustenance. When they left from Los Angeles, they did not have more than their fare to New York. Most of their support came from offerings received while ministering in local meetings along the way. Often, as for so many others, support came from several small donations. Sometimes they would receive only enough in a single meeting to make it to the next leg, where they hoped to garner more support. On rare occasions, however, a single individual would make a large donation to cover a substantial portion of the expense. This was the case for the Batmans. But it was not until the New York meeting that their fare was "all made up" and they received the bulk of the money needed to get them to Africa. A report in *The Apostolic Faith* describes their situation:

> Their faith was severely tested as to their fare. A brother who paid the most of their fare was praying the night before they left that the Lord would give him some revelation. So that night the Lord showed him a lamb that was tied and told him to loose it and as he did so, a great Shekina glory shone in the room. The Lord showed him later that it meant the missionaries he was to be the means of sending on their way.[3]

The Batmans were accustomed to trusting God to supply their sustenance. An article in the December 1906 edition of the newspaper entitled "Mrs. Daisy Batman's Testimony" made this very clear:

> At the age of fourteen, the Lord saved me from my sins. Last April He sanctified my soul, took all inbred sin out and gave me a clean heart fit for the Lord's use. Hallelujah! But still I hungered for more, so when the Pentecost came to Los Angeles, I found that was just what I wanted. But I was working every day and could not be at the meeting much. One day the Lord told me to stop everything and go to the meeting. I said, Lord, I have three small children and no way to support them. He said, I will supply your needs. Glory to God, He has supplied all our needs. We have never needed for anything and have never asked anybody but the blessed Lord for a penny. Three years ago last April, the Lord gave us the call to Africa. At first I thought I would stay and let my husband go, but He said, "No, you must go too." I thought He wanted us to go right away, but when He saw I was willing to spend my life in Africa for precious souls, He revealed to us that He would tell us when to go. And three months after we received our baptism, He said, "Now go to Africa." O glory to God, I am so glad I got to the place where the blessed Lord's will is my will."[4]

Daisy, G. W., and their group stayed in Liverpool for a time and participated in the worship services with Julia Hutchins, Lucy Farrow, and the other Azusa Street missionaries. After a short period the reassembled group departed their separate ways, continuing by steamer to Liberia and Angola.

It is not clear what role Daisy played in the couple's ministry. There appears to be no published reports of her preaching publicly or even praying for converts or seekers of the Holy Spirit baptism. Certainly she shared her testimony of her own Pentecostal experience in the various meetings they conducted. Importantly, however, items in *The Apostolic Faith* generally mention the two of them together, indicating them as the leaders of the mission. Likewise, the Batmans saw themselves as a missionary team, working side-by-side to bring the gospel and news of the Pentecostal blessing to their American audiences and to the continent of Africa. One of the six articles in the December 1906 issue of *Apostolic Faith* spoke of their missionary trip, making it clear that they were a missionary team.

> Bro. and Sister G. W. Batman . . . are tried and true workers and have the enduement of power from on high and the fitness of the gift of tongues. . . . They have the gift of healing and we believe God will wonderfully use them among those darkened souls.[5]

If for no other reason, Daisy Batman deserves mention for the toll exacted from her in following what she perceived to be a God-given call to personally take the message to Africa. The sometime-unrelenting hardship of missionary life was nowhere more evident among Azusa Street workers than among this family. An item in *The Apostolic Faith* was unknowingly prophetic in a description of the Batmans when it asserted, "They started with faith in God though they were taking their three little children, and their destination is called the 'white

man's graveyard'."⁶ During their tour, the entire family—
Daisy, G. W., and their children—contracted black fever, a cur-
able but often fatal disease. All five members of the family succumbed to the disease and died in Africa.

chapter 13

May Evans

A S REPORTED IN *The Apostolic Faith* newspaper, the Azusa Street Revival "began among the colored people" when "God baptized several sanctified wash women with the Holy Ghost, who have been much used of Him."[1] This initial outpouring took place while the revival was still a house meeting in a predominantly black neighborhood in Los Angeles. Though the revival was noted for, among other things, its multiracial worship, it was not until the group reached the Azusa Street location that the racial character of the meetings began to dramatically change. Once there, the meeting grew, and as news of the renewal spread, whites, Latinos, and others were drawn to them.

A small number of whites were hungry enough for a powerful spiritual encounter to traverse the racial divide that characterized American society in the early 1900s. They affiliated with the earliest stage of the revival while it was still at Bonnie Brae Street. Their intense holy desire yielded such spiritual fruit that their testimonies served as the impetus for increasing the participation of other whites.

One of those for whom this social and spiritual investment was to pay personally high dividends was May Evans. Evans was the first white woman to receive the Pentecost and gift of tongues in Los Angeles before the meeting reached Azusa Street.[2]

Most of the information we have about Evans comes from her testimony and several reports about her and her husband, G. W., published in the September, October, November, and December 1906 editions of *The Apostolic Faith*. Indeed, their work is mentioned by name in more editions of the newspaper than that of any other couple.

For several years before coming to Azusa Street, the Evanses were Holiness adherents, and both probably claimed the experience of sanctification. Apparently G. W. was the more prominent preacher among the couple, yet May accompanied him everywhere and actively participated in the meetings he conducted. Newspaper accounts always mention the two as traveling together. Since reports from the revivals and camp meetings highlight the ministry of G. W., we are not sure what role May actually played. But May was also a minister who identified herself as being "in the Lord's work."[3] We do know that William Seymour thought enough of May's spiritual maturity to appoint her as one of the six women who made up the early eleven-member administrative board of the Azusa Street Mission. In this position, she helped oversee the finances of the mission and examined people for ministerial credentials. Seymour also named G. W. as field director, giving him responsibility for overseeing the numerous outside works affiliated with the Azusa Street Mission.

Like so many others who found their way to Azusa Street, May had suffered from a variety of ailments and had undergone numerous medical procedures. Thirteen years before coming to Azusa Street, Evans had already embraced divine healing as part of her Holiness heritage. In a testimony contributed to *The Apostolic Faith,* she graphically recollects her first personal encounter with divine healing:

> I was brought into the light of [d]ivine healing, through the Word of God. I had never heard any teaching from man. But I had been

for a long time very greatly afflicted in body. I had taken physicians and medicine until I became discouraged and continued to grow worse till I decided to drop every remedy and take the Lord for my healer.

To this my people would not give consent. They thought I was losing my mind. One morning, through a nurse, I was chloroformed and taken out of my home to the hospital where they performed an operation. After the physicians had cut and slashed and found that the seat of the trouble was deeper than they anticipated, they lost courage and said it was impossible for me to recover. It was only a question of a few hours that I could possibly live. My husband was away in God's work at the time, and my people became alarmed, and realized what they had done, and decided to take me back to my home to die. But, praise God, He had another plan in store for me.

I did not regain consciousness for many hours, I opened my eyes in my own room and heard them praying around my bed. Then I realized my dreadful situation and in the most excruciating agony, I lifted my eyes to heaven and saw a light streaming down upon me. And in a moment, I heard the voice of Jesus telling me to trust Him, that He was my healer. I said, "Yes, Lord, I do trust Thee and will trust Thee, for Thou hast healed me and healed me now." Then there was a wonderful joy that came into my very being, and I felt the Spirit and the healing power of Christ permeating my whole being, praise God. In three days time I was up and around my room, and in less than a week I was able to walk a mile. Never from that time have I doubted the healing power of Jesus.[4]

Evans enjoyed good health for twelve years after that initial healing. In 1906, however, while on an evangelistic tour with other Azusa faithful, she had an accident that caused her ill health, rectified by a second instance of divine healing. Though this healing did not occur at the Azusa Street Revival, it is indicative of the expectation and experience of the supernatural intervention of God through divine healing that was rife among the Azusa saints. The dramatic testimony was published in the November edition of the newspaper.

> While in Oakland, California, during last August, through an accident, God permitted the old trouble to come back, and from Saturday evening until Tuesday noon, I suffered intensely. At noon time, we always held our workers' class there, and it was during the saints' meeting, I had a wonderful spirit of prayer, and I tried to say, "Jesus is here," and found I had no utterance, but He was present in my soul. The spirit of prayer continued on me until 2:30. When the Lord permitted me to raise my eyes, I saw a vision of beautiful, rolling clouds, and Jesus suspended in the midst, and just then I realized that He was there for my healing. Sister Crawford and Sister Junk who were with me also saw Jesus, and God revealed to them He had come to heal me. I felt the healing work of Jesus. Many of you loved ones have seen the mason lift up his trowel of mo[r]tar and throw it upon the wall that he was building, and just so it seemed to me that the Great Physician was rebuilding the temple of my body. O Hallelujah! Praise His name. O, I know that He is the only physician that can heal all our diseases. All that afternoon and evening, no matter which way I turned, the form of my Savior was suspended in front of me, and I wish ever to behold the smile of His countenance as I saw Him on that day. My healing was instantaneous, and today I rejoice in a perfect body.[5]

The Evanses often traveled with a group of evangelists, called a band, to hold large protracted revival meetings in the cities of the Northwest. On one trip, probably in August 1906, such a band included the Evanses, Florence Crawford, Bro. Johnson, and Louise Condit, who went to Oakland, California, and held a five-week revival in which "sixty-five souls received the baptism with the Holy Ghost, thirty were sanctified and nineteen [were] converted."[6]

A personal testimony from a participant in those meetings, published in the newspaper, described the work of the band and identified G. W. and May Evans and Florence Crawford among those who were conducting the meeting: "When Rev. Evans and his wife and Sister Florence Crawford went to the city of Oakland preaching the full Gospel, I went the first night, . . . when I stepped in, I felt the power of God and could not say that it was the work of the devil, as most of the preachers declared, for I was practically convinced that it was the work of the Holy Ghost."[7]

By November 1906, G. W. and May were, again, part of a group that embarked on a steamer trip to the Northwest, including Oakland, California, Salem, Oregon, and Seattle, Washington. This time the band was made up of Crawford, Brother and Sister Thomas Junk, Sister Ophelia Wiley, and Sister Lulu Miller.[8]

In the latter part of 1906, the Evanses went to Woodland, California, in the northcentral portion of the state. On their return they gave this testimony to the congregation about the results of the Pentecostal revival that was taking place:

Thirty-two have been baptized with the Holy Ghost, thirty-one sanctified, and twenty saved. Seventeen members out of the Baptist Church are filled with the Holy Ghost including the superintendent of the Sunday school and his wife. The Sunday school superintendent of the Methodist Church is also baptized with the Holy Ghost, and the difficulty now on hand is the need of a larger building to accommodate the crowds. Fourteen were healed at one meeting. God's word is made so clear and plain that the crowds are pressing in spiritual hunger for the living truth. . . . A man that had been possessed with a mad demon and had been in the asylum was delivered. The Lord cast out this demon, clothed him in his right mind, and completed the work, baptizing him with the Holy Ghost. Another remarkable case involved a party under sentence of court. The decision was suspended; the defendant was saved, sanctified, and filled with the Holy Ghost and became a good citizen.[9]

chapter 14

Anna Hall

ANNA HALL CAME TO AZUSA STREET armed with a wealth
of ministerial experience. She was a preacher who was
not only an important part of the Azusa Street meetings,
but also had already been an important part of Parham's ministry in Houston and Orchard, Texas. One source asserts that
Hall received the Pentecostal experience prior to joining the
Parham camp, "without hearing the truth except from the
Word."[1] Another insists that she received the experience at a
short-lived prayer meeting in Zion, Illinois,[2] organized by a Mrs.
Waldron, a follower of Parham. In either case, she appeared on
the Azusa Street scene already having experienced the
Pentecostal tongues experience and as a seasoned preacher.

During the early 1900s, Hall was closely affiliated with
Charles Fox Parham and was active in many of his revivals. She
was one of a team of "evangelists"—Parham's students—who
regularly traveled with him to hold meetings and work in the
background as preachers and altar workers. Her gifts and abili-
ties stood out enough above some others that she often shared
the pulpit with Parham and on several occasions was asked to fill
in for him at preaching engagements.

By 1904, Hall was conducting successful meetings for
Parham throughout the Midwest in such cities as Joplin,
Missouri, and Lowell and Lawrence, Kansas. A year later she

ANTA HALL | 129

teamed with Mr. and Mrs. Walter Oyler, whom she had met in Galena, Kansas, while serving in Parham's ministry. Both the Oylers had received the baptism of the Holy Spirit in those services and were anxious to share the experience with friends and family in their hometown. After spending some time working with Parham, they returned to Orchard, Texas, and convinced Hall to accompany them. Once there, Hall rented or bought a home, settled in, and began to minister within the community. Yet, in spite of Hall's being an accomplished preacher, the Oylers and the people they had gathered around them were not satisfied with the results of her meetings and wanted Parham to come and run a revival.

When Parham arrived in Orchard a few weeks later, Hall shared the revival duties with him. It was at an all-day meeting in her home that the first Texans received the Pentecostal baptism. Parham described one service where "Sister Hall and I gave them a rousing talk on victory."[3] He further declared that the revival held in her home was "the grandest witnessed since the outpouring in the Bible school in Topeka." Confident that she could handle the ministry from that point, he returned to Kansas and left Hall to carry on the work in Texas. She continued to minister from her home and to visit new works in the area to encourage and support the workers.

In the summer of 1906, Hall was among fifteen workers who accompanied Parham to Houston to hold camp meetings and street services. In August she reported that she felt God calling her to go to California. Late in that same month she was one of the persons Parham sent to Azusa Street in response to a telegram he received from Seymour telling of the power falling in Los Angeles and asking for additional help. The group prayed, and when they got up, Sister Anna Hall was delegated to go. The necessary funds were immediately laid on the altar and she left for Los Angeles that night.[4] She was accompanied by three of Parham's workers, the Oylers and a Sister Quinton.

After coming to Los Angeles, Hall stayed in contact with Parham, writing to him from time to time about what was going on in the meetings. Probably because of her close affiliation with him, she was shortly involved in making arrangements for his visit and a big meeting of all the saints in which he was expected to participate. For not long after Hall arrived in Los Angeles, William Seymour penned a letter to Parham, saying that "Sister Hall has arrived, and is planning out a great revival in this city that will take place when you come."[5] The big meeting never took place. Once Parham got to Azusa Street, he was appalled by what he considered improper mixing of the races and unsightly behavior of the participants. With Hall's assistance, he set up separate meetings in the city. Though Hall had been an integral part of the Azusa revival, she shared in the YMCA meeting with Parham from that point until they left the city.

In the sermon "Jesus Is Coming," Hall recounts an earlier vision:

A few weeks ago, as we were in our camp meeting, the first night we called our altar service there were 100 at the altar seeking God, and a strange power came into my being that I had felt once before when God wanted to reveal something to me. I have learned that it pays to be quiet before the Lord. I went home to my daughter's house and prepared for bed. Just as the gray dawn began to appear, I waked as if someone had touched my shoulder, and felt the same power. I heard the beautiful warbling of a bird, and thought it was a mocking bird which one might hear there. But no, it seemed away down in my soul. And as that beautiful bird began to sing, I saw a little infant face right before my eyes. And as the song of the bird began to ripple, it began to sound like water running over pebbles. It increased till it sounded like many waters, and the face enlarged till it was a full grown face. I said, "Surely this is a messenger from the holy country." The voice answered. "Yes and I have come to tell you that Jesus is coming. Go forward in My name, preach the Gospel of the Kingdom, for the King's business demands haste. My people have only time to get on the beautiful garments, and prepare for the wedding supper in the Heavens." Dear ones, have you got on the beautiful robes of righteousness? I said, "Lord, reveal unto me what this means, the singing of the bird and rippling of the waters." And God spoke to me, "The singing of the beautiful bird and the baby face was the proclamation of the first coming into the world; and the voice of many waters is the proclamation of Jesus Christ that is soon coming."

Repent and believe the Gospel, for the Kingdom of Heaven is at hand.[6]

An article in the first issue of *The Apostolic Faith* titled "Russians Hear in Their Own Tongue" describes Hall's acumen in the gift of xenolalia. Significantly, she was one of several Azusa Street participants who claimed the ability to speak in known tongues but among the few who actually reported being able to use that gift to minister. She also appears to be among the few who did not see this ability as a sign that they should go as missionaries to a foreign field. Instead, she attempted to use the gift among the immigrant communities that had been among the newer Los Angeles arrivals. As the article put it,

Different nationalities are now hearing the Gospel in their own "tongue wherein they were born." Sister Anna Hall spoke to the Russians in their church in Los Angeles, in their own language as the Spirit gave utterance. They were so glad to hear the truth that they wept and even kissed her hands. They are a very simple, pure, and hungry people for the full Gospel. The other night, as a company of Russians were present in the meeting, Bro. Lee, a converted Catholic, was permitted to speak their language. As he spoke and sang, one of the Russians came up and embraced him. It was a holy sight, and the Spirit fell upon the Russians, as well as on others, and they glorified God.[7]

Another of her sermonic testimonies in the October 1906 issue of *The Apostolic Faith* was entitled "The Polishing Process":

Several years ago, when I was very hungry, seeking God in all His fullness, I shut myself away in my closet one day, and the Lord gave me a wonderful revelation. As I was kneeling before my Maker, beseeching Him to show me all He expected me to be, right before my eyes I saw this wonderful vision. There appeared a man with a large, long, knotty, but straight log. The man had an axe. Did you ever see anybody score timber? He was scoring the log, and it seemed to me the axe went clear to the bit. And every time he scored, it hurt me. He scored it on four sides and then took the broad axe and whacked off the knots. Then he took a line and with adz he made it pretty smooth. Then he raised it in the air, and taking a great plane, turned to me and said: "This is the plane of the Holy Ghost," and he ran the plane up and down, till I could see the image of the man perfectly reflected in the face of the log, as in a mirror. He did this to all four sides. Then turning to me, he said: "Thou art all fair, my love; there is no spot in thee."

That is what God wants to do with us. He wants to take all the bumps, all the barnacles off. We have only begun to lay ourselves on the anvil of God's truth. The hammer is being applied to us. He may have to throw us back in the smelter several times. Let us stay in the fire till there is no more dross in us. Sometimes we think God has done all He needs to do; but something comes up that we do not like, and the old man can get up and hobble off on a pretty good shin.

Several weeks ago, I thought surely the last stroke is put in, and now I am dead to the world. But it was not very long till I found out there was a little self there. I was holding a meeting in a little village. We had to move a kitchen stove, and there was no way but for me to get on top of that cook stove and ride behind an old mule team, and I found Sister Hall had a little life in her yet. Thank God, I am dead to that thing now.

Let us stay on the anvil of God, till we reflect the image of the Master. There is a place where we can get, that God Almighty will say: "Thou art all fair, my love, there is no spot in thee."

—Mrs. Anna Hall.[8]

Her final published sermon, "Honor the Holy Ghost," appeared in the same issue of *The Apostolic Faith*:

Let me warn you, dear ones, as a mother in Israel, don't try to prune one another, Jesus says: "I am the vine and my Father is the husbandman. Every branch in me that beareth not fruit, he purgeth it." Let Him do the pruning and purging. If you see a brother or sister doing anything you do not approve of, instead of blazing it abroad, get down on your knees and say: "My Father, I honor you to bring them out of this fault." Multitudes and great bodies of Christians have gone to the wall for that very same thing. They tried to prune one another, tried to make others believe just as they believed and think just as they thought. If this movement stands for anything, it stands for unity of mind. It was raised up to answer the prayer of Jesus: "That they might be one, as thou Father art in me and I in thee." What is the matter with the world today? Here is a little selfish sect and there a denomination by itself. They do not love one another as God would have them. Let us honor every bit of God there is in one another. Let us honor the Holy Ghost to teach men to get them out of their error. Dear ones, watch and pray that ye enter not into temptation. Watch that something does not come in to grieve the Holy Spirit. "Grieve not the Holy Spirit of God whereby ye are sealed unto the day of redemption."   —Mrs. Anna Hall.[9]

While in Los Angeles, Hall used her gift of languages to preach among Armenians and Russians. She had attended a Russian church in Los Angeles and preached to the congregation in their own language.

Hall went down to the coast of Texas among the French Arcadian Catholics and fishermen, and for two weeks slept on the floor with a pair of blankets under her. Scores of the fishermen were saved through hearing her speak in their language.[10] By November 1906, Brother and Sister Oyler and Brother and Sister Quinton arrived in Los Angeles to minister with Hall in Whittier. The curtain rings down on Hall and we do not hear of her again.

chapter 15

Mabel Witter Smith Hall

THE ONLY PERSONAL INFORMATION we have of Mabel Witter Smith Hall is that she was the daughter of a Galveston physician and, by the time of Parham's Houston revival in 1905, a young widow. She taught school during the day, but in the evenings she could be found working as a member of Parham's team from the first few weeks of his revival meetings. Sometime during this period, she and Parham developed a close father-daughter relationship, and she was to later refer to him as "dear old Daddy."[1]

Smith was uniquely gifted with the ability to not only speak in tongues fluently and interpret but also to understand foreign languages that were naturally being spoken and to respond to them in tongues. Stanley Frodsham, an eyewitness to the events surrounding the Azusa Street outpouring, recounted an incident in which a man walked up to Smith and began speaking in his native German tongue. She answered him back in German, though she had not learned a word of the language.[2]

She was particularly noted for having the gift of xenolalia. The languages that were recognized when she spoke in tongues included Hebrew, German, French, and Spanish. In noting her extraordinary agility with this gift, G. J. Buck, an early observer of Pentecostalism, notes:

> The most fluent and gifted in tongues . . . was . . . a Mrs. Smith . . . [who] never studied languages, a dignified, sensible woman,

as simple as a little child in manner . . . as prayerful and useful a Christian woman as I ever talked with. As I had taught six languages in college, and studied Hebrew some . . . and had therefore some appreciation of the correct sound of language, I enjoyed her talking very much. She did not know one language from another, nor the sound of any language except her own, English. I recognized her German, which she frequently used, her French less often. . . . I have heard her use several different tongues, though her friends said she had spoken seventeen different tongues. Her tongues had been repeatedly translated by passers by, or transient bystanders, who always said she spoke very correctly and sometimes would not believe it was not her native language as it was theirs.[3]

The exuberance of the Pentecost experience often spilled out beyond the confines of worship services in meeting halls. Participants regularly held impromptu, spirited street services in the communities where they lived and on the way to and from the revival meetings. They would share their testimonies in English and tongues with whoever would listen. On more than one occasion, Smith reportedly spoke in tongues while talking on the street. After one street meeting, a man came to her and offered to hire her as an interpreter in his office for those who spoke French and Spanish. He found it incredulous that she did not speak those languages, but the Holy Ghost spoke through her using her tongue.[4] On another occasion, at the close of the Easter anniversary meeting at Orchard, Texas, while waiting for a train, the group launched an impromptu meeting in which Smith preached a sermon in tongues "under the inspiration of the Holy Spirit."[5]

One historian of the movement, Ethel Goss, notes that Smith's gift was particularly useful for witnessing and preaching the gospel in the Mexican Gulf port city of Galveston. Located fifty miles southeast of Houston, it was and is a place where ships from all over the world regularly dock. Their crews spoke a variety of languages. Goss explains that,

> When the group of Pentecostal workers would go to the street service each evening, the crowd which gathered was sure to include some of these visiting sailors. While Mabel was preaching, her language would suddenly change from English into tongues. Sometimes she would preach almost her entire sermon in one foreign language. At other times she would use perhaps as many as three or four. Always there was someone in the audience who understood what she was saying, and after the service would want to talk with her in his native tongue.[6]

Smith had been a close associate of Goss' husband and his first wife Millicent. The trio had met through their mentor, Charles Parham. In 1905, Parham sent a group, including Smith, to follow up on his initial contacts in Zion City, Illinois, and to hold a revival in that city. Parham himself did not make the first of two extended visits to Zion City until 1906. By then, Smith and other workers had set the climate for an extended revival by their diligence there. Though Parham was certainly the leader in these meetings, he afforded Smith and others the opportunity to preach. One of the participants in the Zion City revival remembers Mabel Smith's role:

> How preciously anointed she was! We can still feel the thrill of her messages, not because they were worldly-wise, but as the Spirit would come upon her a beautiful glow would suffuse her face, and words poured from her lips as from a fountain. Always there was a message in tongues, with the interpretation, and the room was filled with the presence of the Holy One. Quiet and reserved, this sister was the means of blessing and help to many in those seeking days.[7]

We do not know when Smith arrived at Azusa Street or how long she stayed, but by the time of her arrival sometime in 1906 she had considerable ministry experience and was already baptized in the Holy Spirit with the Pentecostal evidence of tongues.

Smith left Azusa Street in the fall of 1906 to respond to a call for help from a former follower of Alexander Dowie,[8] who had relocated to Chelsea, Massachusetts. On their way east, Smith and her husband Jesse preached nightly to "overflowing crowds" in Chicago. It was Smith's ministry in that city that convinced William Durham, prominent pastor of North Avenue Mission, to visit the Los Angeles revival. This invitation set up a chain of events that led to one of the first major schisms in the fledgling movement.

Yet, even after visiting Azusa Street, Smith's loyalties remained with Parham. By 1907, Smith had migrated to Massachusetts where she was attempting to arrange for Charles Parham to come and hold a revival meeting.[9]

Her testimony and ministry was instrumental in convincing at least two prominent Holiness leaders, Samuel Gottis of the Christian Workers Union, and Morton Plummer, editor of *Word and Work,* to embrace the Pentecostal movement. Sometime later she married Lemuel Hall, a West Point graduate and also the son of a physician and the grandson of a governor of Alabama, who Alex Bills refers to as possibly the best educated and most "silver tongued" preacher among the early leaders.[10] Smith herself had only completed a high school education.

Mabel Smith Hall died sometime before 1922, for H. G. Tuthill, who calls her a bright and shining light, declares of her in his 1922 work that "The Lord . . . used her for His glory [only a few] years then called her home to himself."[11]

chapter 16

Ivy Glenshaw Campbell

IVY GLENSHAW CAMPBELL HOLDS TWO distinctions among the women of Azusa Street. First, she was the first white woman to have the experience of speaking in tongues once the revival reached Azusa Street. Secondly, she was largely responsible for the spread of the Pentecostal movement to Ohio and Pennsylvania. Called Iva by her close friends and associates, Campbell was a seamstress by trade. She had been reared with two sisters in a strict Presbyterian home in East Liverpool, Ohio, a community forty-seven miles south of Youngstown, bordering western Pennsylvania. As a young woman, she had faithfully attended and supported her Presbyterian church.

In 1901, while still living in East Liverpool, she reported having experienced sanctification as a second work of grace. Her pastor roundly denounced her declaration of this experience since it was theologically at odds with a Calvinist understanding of the mode of salvation. Campbell found herself ostracized by fellow worshipers and was forced to leave the congregation. She then joined with other Holiness associates to form the Broadway Mission in 1902. Campbell promptly became a leader in that congregation.

By 1906, Campbell was thirty-two years old and had migrated to California. She was a member of the Eighth and Maple Avenue Mission in Los Angeles, pastored by William Pendleton. Pendleton and his members were among the Holiness groups who embraced the Pentecostal message. He and several members of his congregation had begun attending the Azusa revival and received Holy Spirit baptism by mid-June. On one occasion, Campbell came with them and started seeking the Holy Spirit baptism. She received her Pentecostal experience in July 1906. Though many of the congregants who came with Pendleton eventually found a home back at his mission. Campbell stayed at Azusa Street, involved herself in outreach work, and made a home for herself in one of the back apartments.

Campbell was one of those who claimed the gift of xenolalia and insisted that she could speak in both Chinese and a Central African dialect. On one occasion, she was teaching a class of Chinese children when she began to speak in tongues. She claimed that at least one child recognized the language and responded to her in the same dialect. On another occasion, Campbell spoke in tongues in a worship service, and a missionary from Central Africa identified the language as one spoken in his region.

From Azusa Street, Campbell wrote about her experiences and the ongoing revival in a letter to pastor Claude A. McKinney of the Union Gospel Mission in Akron, Ohio. McKinney desired to visit the revival but was dissuaded by his wife from undertaking such a long trip. Instead, he waited anxiously for Campbell's return to Ohio to receive a firsthand account of the experiences of the Azusa Street Revival.

Campbell set out for Ohio in November 1906 with Thomas Sargent and Margaret Miller, thus making her the first person to bring the Pentecostal revival to the state. Therefore, William

Seymour issued her credentials as a "missionary" in the Apostolic Faith Movement. He also laid hands on her and prayed for the success of her ministry. The first act did two things. First, it assured that Campbell could attain the reduced fares allotted for ministers who traveled by rail and put the official stamp on her affiliation with the Azusa Street Mission. The second was considered an essential impartation of power for the spiritual success of any venture taken on by those going out from Azusa Street.

Campbell's first stop in Ohio was in her hometown of East Liverpool. She had hoped and expected to receive a warm welcome from the Holiness congregation she had helped establish and lead. Instead, the congregation did not welcome her with open arms. On the one hand, she received a lukewarm response to her message regarding the Pentecostal experience, and a controversy ensued that threatened to split the congregation. Not interested in seeing that happen, Campbell moved on. She maintained her residence in East Liverpool as a home base and held revival meetings in Akron, Alliance, and Cleveland, Ohio. She took her message throughout the Pittsburgh area and to Springboro, Pennsylvania.

On the other hand, McKinney and the rest of the saints in Akron saw her trip and ministry as an answer to their prayer for the Pentecostal outpouring. McKinney quickly invited her to hold services in his church, and she promptly accepted. By the end of December, the revival was underway. Midway through the meeting, a report was sent to the saints at Azusa Street from an unnamed participant.

Since I heard of the wonderful way God was working in Los Angeles, my heart got hungry, and the dear saints in Akron kept up a steady cry to God day and night for Him to send it this way. And before we hardly knew it, Akron was visited. Glory to God! He sent dear Ivy Campbell here in answer to prayer, and many have received their Pentecost. The altar is more than filled nearly every service. In fact there is hardly a break in the meeting. Some people bring lunches and don't stop to eat them. Some of the sisters sing in tongues like voices from heaven and also interpret some. O, it is wonderful! Many demons have been cast out and the sick are being healed. Glory to Jesus! He is also selecting His missionaries. The meeting runs day and night—sometimes all night.

People come from miles around here and are receiving their personal Pentecost. Bro. McKinney is sending out invitations far and near, and telling how God is visiting Akron; and it brings in the hungry ones. His church doors were opened wide to welcome dear Sisters Iv[e]y Campbell and Hudson from East Liverpool. The meetings have been running over three weeks. The Holy Ghost is the only leader. Praise God!

While some of the prominent ministers are opposing it, yet their hungry members jump over the fence and get to the little mission church and get saved, sanctified, and then receive their personal Pentecost. We are glad God had one humble preacher in Akron who opened wide the door to receive this "latter rain." We are likely just getting the first sprinkling of the great shower that is to come. Praise God! The burden of everyone that has received their personal Pentecost is "Jesus is coming soon."[1]

The meeting in Akron lasted more than seven weeks and ended in February 1907. It drew people from more than four states. Many came in response to notes that Pastor McKinney excitedly sent out to tell them about the revival and what he saw as a mighty move of God. He invited them to come see for themselves what God was doing. These meetings were also widely reported in the secular press within the region, drawing a mixture of curiosity, awe, and criticism. Attendance grew to the point that crowds of people had to be turned away, and the police were needed to keep order.

Campbell's ministry in Akron and other places drew not only regular seekers but prominent pastors and evangelists of that day coming from throughout the eastern United States. They sat under her ministry and were baptized with the Spirit, then went out to spread the Pentecostal message throughout the East Coast. Levi Lupton, a radical evangelist and pastor in the Ohio Yearly Friends Meeting, was among those who were the fruit of Campbell's ministry. Lupton pastored the First Friends Church in Alliance, Ohio, and ran a training school for missionaries. He and several of his students attended Campbell's meetings. The spiritual fervor that they took from her revival sparked Lupton and his colleagues to wholeheartedly embrace the Pentecostal message.

J. E. Sawders, an independent itinerant Wesleyan Holiness evangelist, was another who sat under Campbell's ministry. Once receiving his Pentecostal baptism, Sawders picked up Campbell's message and carried it to Cleveland. His ministry prompted the same level of controversy from both the secular press and the clergy as they did of his mentor.

Campbell's own assessment of her labors is carried in a correspondence from her dated January 22, 1907, that appeared in an article entitled "Report From Ohio and Pennsylvania," printed in the February 1907 issue of *The Apostolic Faith*:

The battle is on and the devil is surely howling, but O how sweet Jesus keeps me in the midst of it all. We are en-route for Pittsburgh, Pennsylvania. Some of the Akron workers have gone and have great victories there or near there in Homestead, Pennsylvania, a suburban town. We have been invited to many of the Christian Missionary Alliance homes and Missions.

At Akron, Ohio, the meetings have been going on night and day since Dec. 5. People are coming from all around, Indiana, Michigan, Pennsylvania, and other places.

Rev. Lupton who is in charge of the work here is a Friends minister, a very holy, devoted man of God. He has a Missionary Training School or home built for the purpose of sending workers into the harvest, full-fledged Apostolic workers. The school had been going on for three years, and he had been teaching more than he had really experienced. Hearing of the work at Akron, he with eight or ten students came, accepted the teaching, tarried nine days, and received his Pentecost. He speaks in five different languages. Eight of the students and some others have also received the baptism with the Holy Ghost.

Bro. Lupton makes the proposition that we use the home here for a headquarters for the Middle States. I feel it is of God and a good thing, as the Akron work and this is one. They can go on a street car from one place to the other. The home has 14 rooms, I think. In the upper room furnished for a classroom, many have received their Pentecost. The Akron paper, "Pentecostal Wonders" has been consolidated with Bro. Lupton's paper, "The New Acts." The home here is three miles out of the city of Alliance, God's chosen spot where people can come from Cleveland, Akron, and Canton.

They have a large camp ground here, tents and everything to push out into the great battle for God. Many are fighting to the bitter end, but God is raising up precious workers to push the work. One young student got through last night in the basement fixing the furnace, putting in coal. I met him in the hall and he told how he had received the Holy Ghost in the cellar. We had a great time praising God.[2]

Campbell's evaluation of the fruit of the revival in the Midwest was substantiated by an influx of reports to a number of Pentecostal publications throughout northern and eastern Ohio and western Pennsylvania. These heightened the excitement with which the revival was received by highlighting the miraculous nature of her meetings.

From Cleveland, Ohio:

We are having great victory here. Have been here more than a week. The fire is falling. Many getting through. Nine received Pentecost this week. I came just for one day but God is holding me.

From Canton, Ohio:

Fire is falling at Canton, Ohio. At least seven at that place have received their baptism at Bro. Rohrer's mission. Deep conviction. The stoutest hearts slain under the power. Sinners coming home to God.

From Pittsburgh, Pennsylvania:

We have been holding services in the South Side Mission for the last three weeks steadily every night. Prayer has been answered and four of the seeking ones have received their Pentecost and speak in a strange language. One boy twelve or fourteen years old, speaks Italian very distinctly, and interprets in English. The sisters speak sentences and quote texts of Scripture, and sing in the language they have received and interpret. Two of the sisters have the same tongue and when one begins to sing some hymn, the other starts in and voices the same words.

From Akron, Ohio:

A Methodist minister from another part of the state received his baptism with the Bible evidence. Bro. and Sister Welch . . . have just received their Pentecost. The Spirit whispered to him that God also had touched his eyes, and he found it was so, being able to read without glasses. One lady had said to Bro. McKinney, "I have become almost discouraged. I have been seeking so long without receiving." A night or two afterwards, when the special revival meetings commenced in her church, she went forward to help and pray with the seekers for pardon of purity, when somewhat to her surprise as well as that of others, the baptism came and she began speaking among them in a new language. A returned missionary from India has very recently received the intense desire of her heart at Akron, and the Spirit has spoken through her in attestation of the baptism.

From Potterbrook, Pennsylvania:

Praise God, the Holy Ghost came today. A minister slain under the power. Demons cast out of many. Then Pentecost fell, and ten persons came through with stammering lips and other tongues. Rev. Robbins speaking in a clear language, the Spirit also sang through him. One lady speaking in tongue said. "Jesus is coming." Real Pentecost. Praise God.

Two items were reported by Pastor J. E. Sawders in Homestead, Pennsylvania. The first appeared with the group above, all of which were excerpted from *New Acts:*

We are sweeping this place for God now. Yesterday afternoon, we had a most remarkable service. Rev. J. T. Body lay for hours under the power, and then began to speak clearly and fluently in a new tongue. A man who heard him speak last night told the audience that it was the Hebrew language. He has a marvelous experience.

A young woman was rescued Sunday morning from the police station, went to the altar and was converted Sunday night, was sanctified Monday afternoon and testified to having a pure heart. And Monday night, after lying under the power was baptized with the Holy Ghost and spoke distinctly in a new and flowing language. The lady who rescued her, came through at the same time, and spoke much in Spanish, which I easily understood. The congregation sat and listened in amazement, in the presence of the wonderful operations of the Spirit of God.

A young preacher named McNight, who sat in a large chair under the power, gave out some indistinct utterances, then broke out in a flow of High German, and I understood absolutely every word he uttered. It was wonderful to me. It seemed to me almost as if he had learned the language in which he had spoken so fluently and clearly, so I asked him if he could speak German, and he said No. He is either of Irish or Scotch ancestry.

The meetings go on every day from 2 P.M. until 12 and 1 A.M. Last night the new hall 22 by 70 was well filled. We began with testimonies, when the power came upon us so that there was no opportunity to speak or even read a verse of Scripture. They began coming to the altar, largely young men, and filled two 16 foot altars, then all the front seats. The power was so irresistible that people fell from their seats until the floor was literally covered with prostrate people. One man got the baptism in his home and speaks in a tongue. This makes eight or ten at this date, and scores are seeking at every service.[3]

The second of Sawders' reports in the same issue, entitled "Demons Cast Out," was billed as an "account of a Spiritualist being saved and sanctified."

We have had some of the most wonderful experiences with demons that I have ever seen in my life. One woman, a Spiritualist, from the age of sixteen, was possessed with a legion of demons. The devil threw her on the floor where she fought and foamed froth out of her mouth, saying, "I hate Jesus Christ," many times, and blasphemed God in the most diabolic manner possible to imagine. She pointed right up in the faces of those praying for her, with a hellish laugh, challenging and defying God Almighty, saying, "Ha! ha! She is mine, ha! ha! She belongs to me," etc. Well, we prayed in Jesus name till she was gloriously delivered, and settled down like a lamb at the feet of Jesus, and for hours prayed and praised Him, until He forgave her, then cleansed her heart, and since then she has been seeking Pentecost. Last night she got up and told her whole experience, and it was simply wonderful indeed. She is very intelligent and she now feels that God is going to use her for revenge upon the devil and his hellish work in Spiritualism. These cities are full of Spiritualists and no doubt God will use this woman now to expose the thing from an experimental standpoint.[4]

The success of these individual meetings prompted leaders to form alliances to host regional camp meetings to continue promoting the spirit of revival. The notice for one such event planned for Ohio appeared in the February 1907 issue of *The Apostolic Faith:* "A convention of Prayer is to be held at Alliance, Ohio. The saints from Akron, Cleveland, Canton, and East Liverpool will meet there, and it will no doubt be a time of great power and blessing. The date is March 30th."[5]

In June 1907, Campbell and McKinney joined with Levi Lupton to hold a Pentecostal camp meeting in Alliance, Ohio, which Pentecostal historians assert had a major impact on the spread of the movement in the Northeast. More than seven hundred people attended from twenty-one states and Canada. Among the attendees were many who would go on to become leaders in the Pentecostal movement, such as Roswell Flower, pioneer leader in the Assemblies of God who founded the periodical *The Pentecostal Evangel,* and Joseph King, founder and first bishop of the Pentecostal Holiness Church.

While Campbell was in Ohio, Frank Bartleman, an eyewitness historian for the Azusa Street Revival and itinerant evangelist and pastor, invited her to preach in his meeting. He asserted that Campbell had been sent ahead to prepare the way for his own message.[6]

Later that summer, Campbell, Lupton, McKinney, and their associates organized a camp meeting at Beulah Park campground in Cleveland, Ohio. This location is where many of the ministers and laity of the Christian and Missionary Alliance came into the Pentecostal experience. Some of these later aligned themselves with the Assemblies of God. Others remained with the alliance, somewhat modifying their views on speaking in tongues to conform to the alliance's position on that subject.

Not everyone was enamored with Campbell's ministry. Just as with other Azusa Street outposts, controversy ensued among both the religious and secular communities. The secular press started first. The *Los Angeles Times* article, which described Campbell simply as "a large woman with a mass of chestnut hair," derided many aspects of the services she conducted, paying particular attention to the involvement of "young white girls acting like Negroes" and the use of tongues. It also took this opportunity to castigate the entire Azusa Street movement, sarcastically reporting that "News of the success of Campbell reached the meeting at Azusa Street last night. Excitement was intensified when Seymour was reported to have declared that she had been responsible for fifty souls being saved in Akron, Ohio."[7]

Pastors in the area were quick to comment on the stories in the secular press and the questions they spawned among their parishioners. One clergy member asserted Campbell's meetings were a fraud. Another asserted that Campbell preached a "ridiculously insane doctrine" that was "sacrilegious," an "irreparable evil," and a "libel on religion."[8] Among the harshest critiques was a comparison of occurrences at Campbell's meetings with the outbreak of hysteria and hypnotic extravagance that led to the Salem Witch Trials.[9]

At first Campbell ignored the criticism. But finally, when it reached a point of severity she could no longer tolerate, she denounced the press from the pulpit, threatening them with "the curse of God" for their ridicule.[10]

Campbell never married. Reportedly, she had expected to eventually serve as a missionary to Africa. A. A. Boddy, publisher of *Confidence*, reported that when he saw her in 1912 at Azusa Street, she appeared to be in poor health. She spent the last two years of her life in California. Reportedly, like the Seymours and Lucy Farrow, she lived in one of the small apartments above the mission after returning from Ohio. She died there in 1918 at the age of forty-four.

PART FOUR

The Afterglow of the Revival

*B*y most estimations, the Azusa Street Revival ended by 1914 even though the mission continued holding worship services into the 1930s. With its end, an unprecedented period of gender and racial equality also came to an end. It was never to be repeated within Pentecostalism or any other sector of evangelical Christianity. The period following the revival was to see initially a slow, then more dramatic decline in the leadership of women in the Pentecostal movement. Yet, a few women continued to play important roles, and several women had major impacts on the continued growth of Pentecostalism.

The Pentecostal fire did not go out with the revival. It continued to burn sometimes dimly, sometimes brightly in dispersed pockets throughout the nation and the world. And the women who had been at Azusa Street continued to be sparks, igniting new flames and rekindling embers of revival wherever they found themselves.

As for Azusa Street—the place where the revival started—it eventually became little more than a dim flame. After William Joseph Seymour's death, little more than a handful of the faithful remained at the homefront, carrying on worship services whenever they could. They were presided over by his widow, Jennie Evans Seymour, who continued to stoke the fading embers as long as she could. But their efforts were to fail in the midst of controversy and financial hardship. The mission would be closed and later torn down. For years it did not even have a plaque to commemorate its importance.

Though the revival and home were gone, they were never entirely forgotten due to the efforts of one woman. Emma Cotton's attempt to rekindle the memory of the original flame was launched on two fronts. Thirty years after the initial revival began, she published the "Message of the Apostolic Faith" to keep the memory of the revival fresh in the minds of the saints who had been there and introduce it to a new generation who had only heard the stories. She endeavored to reignite the passion of the old revival by holding commemorative services that would take many of the old saints back to their roots and introduce a new generation to revival—Azusa Street style.

The Azusa Street message and spirit would eventually find a solid place in American religion through the establishment of several Pentecostal denominations who trace their roots back to the revival. Commonly, people learned about the revival through the men who eventually came to assume denominational leadership. The Assemblies of God would be one such denomination. Men such as Howard Goss, Mack Pinson, and J. Roswell Flower, who were to become important leaders in the denomination, all had a direct or indirect tie to the Azusa Street Revival.

But the Assemblies had another unique link to the revival. Though Rachel Harper Sizelove held no official position in the denomination, she established several works that became important congregations within the denomination. More importantly, she is credited for having a divine revelation of the exact location for the headquarters of the denomination that has arguably grown to be the largest Pentecostal body in the world. The contributions of these women are excellent examples of the kinds of secondary roles women were later to play in the movement—one that has been easy to overlook by many Pentecostal historians.

chapter 17

Jennie Evans Moore Seymour

JENNIE EVANS MOORE was perhaps the most influential woman in the life and ministry of William Joseph Seymour, the founder of the Azusa Street Mission and leader of the revival. Initially a minor player in its unfolding, she first encountered the people who became major and minor players in the revival as an onlooker. Through a series of providential "circumstances," quickly became a part of this amazing movement that was finally to consume her undying loyalty. She was ultimately to become Seymour's wife, most intimate confidante and supporter, as well as the leader of the remnant who remained faithful to the mission after his death.

Jennie Evans Moore was born in Austin, Texas, on March 10, 1874, to Jackson and Eliza Moore. She was described by A. A. Boddy, editor of *Confidence*, as a "bright coloured Christian" and an "intelligent Negro sister."[1] She was also characterized as a powerful and interesting speaker and a beautiful singer. Reportedly when asked, she gave her race as Ethiopian.

Nothing is recorded of Jennie's early education or family life. Nor do we have information on her religious background, but her link to the revival began several months before it actually got underway. In early 1906 Moore was employed as a cook and housekeeper for the Walter Cline family, who were influential, white, and based in Los Angeles. She and her family lived at 217 Bonnie Brae Street, located directly across the street from the 214 Bonnie Brae Street cottage where Julia Hutchins and her little Holiness congregation had a temporary home and had launched an evangelistic outreach throughout the neighborhood. Jennie was won to faith through this outreach and for a time was a member of Hutchins' congregation.

Sometime between Moore's conversion by Hutchins' group and her joining Seymour's group, Hutchins' congregation moved to new quarters. During that time Moore frequented worship services at Joseph Smale's New Testament Church. When Seymour was locked out of Hutchins' church and moved to the Bonnie Brae home, Moore was attracted to the prayer meeting and started attending in the evenings, though presumably she still attended Smale's services on Sunday mornings.

On an evening in April 1906, as the meetings got underway in earnest on Bonnie Brae Street and revival fires began to ignite, Moore was praying with others in the Asberry house. Brother Lee came out of his house, ran down the street, and burst in to the room. Farrow and Seymour had just laid hands on him to receive his Holy Spirit baptism, and his excitement was contagious. As he came through the door with his hands raised, speaking in tongues, Moore spontaneously joined in with her own new tongue. Several others in the room quickly shared the same experience. Through this episode, Jennie Moore became the first person at the 214 Bonnie Brae Street address, and both the first woman and the second person to receive the experience of the baptism of the Holy Spirit with tongues before the revival moved to Azusa Street.

At the time Moore received her Pentecostal experience, she was sitting on an organ stool though she was not a musician. Her perch there was to have prophetic significance that would become apparent as the evening events unfolded. Moore reportedly fell to the floor and began speaking six distinctive languages. In the midst of this exuberant experience, she was reminded of a vision she had several months earlier. Each language she spoke was accompanied by an interpretation in English. In her own words, she recounts the vision and her revelation of its meaning:

> For years before this wonderful experience came to us, we as a family were seeking to know the fullness of God, and He was filling us with His presence until we could hardly contain the power. I had never seen a vision in my life, but one day as we prayed, there passed before me three white cards, each with two names thereon, and but for fear I could have given them, as I saw every letter distinctly. On April 9, 1906, I was praising the Lord from the depths of my heart at home, and when the evening came and we attended the meeting the power of God fell and I was baptized in the Holy Ghost and fire, with the evidence of speaking in tongues. During the day I had told the Father that although I wanted to sing under the power I was willing to do what ever He willed, and at the meeting when the power came on me I was reminded of the three cards which had passed me in the vision months ago. As I thought thereon and looked to God, it seemed as if a vessel broke within me and water surged up through my being, which when it reached my mouth came out in a torrent of speech in the languages which God had given me. I remembered the names of the cards: French, Spanish, Latin, Greek, Hebrew, Hindustani, and as the message came with power, so quick that

but few words would have been recognized, interpretation of each message followed in English, the name of the language would come to me. . . .[2]

The prophetic character of her earlier perch became evident as she went to the piano and began playing it, singing and praying in tongues, though she had never had a piano lesson and, prior to that evening, had never played the piano. Again, in her own words,

> I sang under the power of the Spirit in many languages, the interpretation both words and music which I had never before heard, and in the home where the meeting was being held, the Spirit led me to the piano, where I played and sang under inspiration, although I had not learned to play.[3]

After the others in the meeting began to speak in tongues, Moore ran out onto the front porch and began to prophesy in Hebrew. No doubt her exhibition was one of the occurrences that began to draw neighbors to the meetings.

While her dramatic experience with the piano was unique, it was also exemplary of the fervor that attended these meetings. The small group of primarily black women household workers had come every morning and evening—whenever their work schedule would allow—seeking a deeper experience of God, and they found it.

One story about Moore occurred several days after her baptism. She was going about her work as a household maid, assisting her employer in serving a Good Friday dinner party. After the meal was served, Moore and her employer were in a discussion about some household issue when Moore spontaneously began to speak fluently in tongues. The woman was frightened by the experience; thinking that Moore might be suffering from a mental collapse, she insisted that Jennie take off a week to rest.[4]

While the revival still remained at Bonnie Brae Street for a short period, Moore was among the first to take the news of the revival to the broader Los Angeles Christian community. On Easter Sunday in 1906, Moore attended worship services at Joseph Smale's First New Testament Church. At the close of the service, when a space was allotted for personal testimonies, Moore seized the opportunity to tell about the prayer meeting at Bonnie Brae Street and her experience of speaking in tongues. Following her testimony in English, she immediately began to speak fluently in tongues. Neighbor Ruth Asberry, who was hosting the meeting in her home, had accompanied Moore to the services. When Moore stopped speaking, Asberry immediately gave an English interpretation of Moore's message: "This is that which was spoken of by the prophet Joel."[5]

Though this was a Holiness congregation that was used to outbreaks of religious fervor, reaction to this display was mixed. Some in the congregation considered Moore's conduct excessive and fanatical. Others had their interest pricked and were drawn to the cottage prayer meeting to see for themselves what was going on. They brought others with them, and so the meeting began to grow.

As the revival moved from Bonnie Brae Street to Azusa Street and developed a little more structure, the band of volunteers who surrounded William Seymour took on a number of volunteer ministry tasks. Moore was among those who regularly assisted at the Azusa Street Mission. Within the worship services, Moore led singing and played the piano. She was also one of the women who served on the administrative board responsible for examining ministers for credentials, and she was eventually appointed a city evangelist along with Phoebe Sergeant.

Moore became a preacher in her own right and has been described as a powerful and interesting speaker, even though her own assessment of herself was that she was simply "a witness for Him under the power of the Holy Ghost."[6] Between 1907 and 1908 when she was not at the Azusa Street Mission, Jennie was itinerating as an evangelist, speaking to large and small congregations throughout the West and Midwest. Like the others who went out from the mission, she regularly filed reports. An item in *The Apostolic Faith* briefly describes a revival she held at William Durham's North Avenue Mission in Chicago: "Sister Jennie E. Moore . . . ha[s] been working in Chicago and other places, writes: 'Truly, beloved, the mission . . . is a blessed place—many Spirit-filled men and women and children. They have more children than at Azusa and they are filled. Beloved, I wish you could see them.'"[7]

In May 1908, a little more than two years after the revival began, William Seymour married Jennie Evans Moore in a private ceremony conducted by his friend and colleague, Edward Lee. Richard Asberry, the host of the Bonnie Brae Street meetings, and Lee's wife Mattie served as witnesses. The marriage set off a controversy that proved to have ongoing consequences for the future of the ministry of the Azusa Street Mission.

Prior to the marriage, Seymour sensed that strong opposition might come from two directions The first was lodged at marriage in general and would come from those within the Holiness movement who contended that the imminent return of Christ left no room for involvement in such "worldly" pursuits as marriage. These things, they demanded, detracted from efforts to win as many of the lost as possible. The other would be specifically lodged at this marriage, and it would come from Seymour's close friend and associate Clara Lum. Lum was a white woman who, despite the racial morays of that day, reportedly felt that Seymour might marry her. And reportedly, Seymour had considered such a liaison. However, once he consulted with his counselors, he was dissuaded from making such a move for fear that it might prove disastrous for the ministry.

To head off the general opposition, Seymour preached a series of messages about marriage and printed an article in *The Apostolic Faith* concerning the issue. In the article entitled "Bible Teaching on Marriage and Divorce," he adamantly declared, "It is no sin to marry."⁸ In a sermon entitled "The Marriage Tie," he further insisted, "[Marriage] is honorable in all," and "[t]he forbidding of marriage is a doctrine of devils."⁹ There was nothing he could do to alleviate the hurt feelings from the second source of opposition. Subsequently, Lum left the Azusa Street Mission and moved to Portland, where she worked with Florence Crawford.

After the marriage, the couple moved into a modest apartment above the mission, though Jennie continued to own a home on Bonnie Brae Street. Reportedly, the couple adopted a daughter, but nothing is known about the girl. Some sources suggest that she later became a part of the Church of God in Christ.

With the marriage, Jennie played an ever-expanding role in the leadership of the mission. She regularly preached in the worship services, filled in for Seymour as pastor when he was away, and occasionally traveled on his behalf. From time to time she also accompanied him when he traveled and was with him when he went to Oregon to confront Crawford and Lum about *The Apostolic Faith* mailing list.

Despite the friction that existed between some in both Crawford's and Seymour's camps, the two groups maintained close relations for some time. In October 1909, only several months after Crawford left Los Angeles for the last time, Jennie Seymour co-signed for the Articles of Incorporation for her Portland organization. Presumably, relations between the Seymours and Crawford had not been strained to their end.

Between 1910 and 1922, the waning years of the Azusa Street Mission, Jennie Seymour served at the helm of leadership with her husband William over the small faithful remnant and became more involved in the decision-making process. It was probably during this time that William made Jennie the only woman member of the official board of trustees for the mission. It was also during this period the couple traveled together to the various camp meetings in which William was invited to speak.

In 1911, Seymour and his wife visited Crawford to request that the newsletter mailing list be returned to them. It was not. In that same year, Jennie invited William Durham to preach a series of messages that proved to be detrimental to the health of the mission. This invitation proved to have disastrous effects for an already tenuous situation. Durham openly denounced Seymour's understanding of the doctrine of entire sanctification that had been the lynchpin of Holiness-Pentecostal theology. In its place, he introduced the doctrine of the finished work of Calvary.[10] The resulting schism saw a number of Seymour's congregation defect to embrace Durham's teaching.

By 1917, the declining attendance and finances at the mission made it necessary for Jennie to return to the secular workforce. She had to help augment the dwindling family resources that resulted from a decline in the Azusa Street Mission and in William's influence among his Pentecostal brethren. Though some in the movement still esteemed him highly, the offerings, preaching engagements, and the honorariums that might accompany them were, presumably, becoming less available to the couple.

Sources suggested that from the beginning, Jennie Seymour was less trusting of white people and less optimistic about the prospect of true racial harmony within the movement than was her husband. Some suggest that she was a source of agitation among the white members of the congregation and that this led to further decline in the membership of the mission. None of this, however, lessened William's trust in his wife.

Before William Seymour died in 1922, he placed the leadership of the ministry in his wife's hands. At his death, Jennie assumed the pastorate over the even smaller remnant. During her tenure as pastor, the ministry initially withstood several blows that were ultimately to prove fatal to its very existence. First, in 1930, she and the congregation were successful in withstanding an attempt by R. C. Griffith to take over the ministry and replace her as pastor. Griffith, a white man, claimed to be a Coptic priest. The resulting battle was resolved in the courts, with Jennie Seymour retaining leadership of the group. The legal proceedings, however, were costly for the small congregation, and most of the few remaining white members sided with Griffith and left.[11]

Unfortunately, the group could not withstand the resulting financial problems that beset the ministry. After having lived in the upstairs apartment since her 1931 marriage to William, Jennie was forced to vacate the building, as it had been condemned by the city of Los Angeles as a fire hazard. She moved her small, beleaguered congregation of the last faithful few into her home on Bonnie Brae Street—coming almost full circle to the location where the revival began. She continued to hold worship services there until her health failed in 1933. At one point, Pastor Seymour mortgaged her home, attempting to save the mission. She later sold the mortgages on the mission and her home to a Los Angeles bank. When she could no longer make payments, the bank foreclosed on the mission, and the building was razed.

Jennie Evans Seymour died in 1936 at the age of sixty-two, three years after she relinquished leadership of the church. She had served as pastor over an increasingly dwindling congregation for fourteen years. With her death, the ministry of Azusa Street ended, and with it, the legacy of women's leadership in the life and ministry of the mission came to an end.

chapter 18

Emma Cotton

EMMA COTTON CAME TO
AZUSA STREET in the first
year of the revival, attracted by what she later was to refer
to as "word of the great awaken-
ing of the Spirit."[1] While one historian places her involvement in
the revival as early as the Bonnie
Brae Street prayer meeting, we
are not sure what role she played
there or once the revival reached
Azusa Street. We are sure that
she was an active participant
who received her Pentecostal
experience during the revival.

Cotton was born in Louisiana in 1877 and was of Creole
descent. At the time of the revival, Emma's husband Henry was
a railroad cook who served the route between Los Angeles and
San Antonio, Texas. Though both were in the ministry, his busy
work schedule left Emma with abundant time to travel around
Southern California and itinerate as an evangelist.

Like so many other women and men attracted to the revival,
Cotton had suffered from several physical illnesses that plagued
her for years, including "weak lungs" and cancer of the nose. She

regularly consumed so many medications to stabilize these conditions that she described herself as having been a "walking drugstore." Also, like the others, Cotton not only received her Pentecostal experience at the revival, but she received healing from all of her conditions.

For thirty years following the revival, we lose track of Cotton except to know that she was involved in evangelistic preaching throughout California, including holding a divine healing service at the Pentecostal Assembly in San Jose. She probably confined her ministry primarily to that state and planted congregations in Fresno, Bakersfield, and Oakland before settling in Los Angeles, though she also did some evangelistic work back in Louisiana.

When we pick up her story again in the 1930s, Cotton had become one of the few women who were friends with evangelist Aimee Semple McPherson, founder of the five-thousand-member Angelus Temple and the International Church of the Foursquare Gospel, one of the major Pentecostal denominations. McPherson was notorious for, among other things, her inability to get along with other women leaders and rarely allowed a woman to grace her pulpit. Cotton was an exception to this rule, and she was also among a small number of women who McPherson allowed to preach at Angelus Temple. On several occasions she and her husband Henry shared what had become one of the most visible pulpits in the Pentecostal movement. To preach there was attestation to both McPherson's esteem for the Cottons and the generally high estimation in which their preaching was held by others in the Pentecostal movement.

In 1936, Cotton led a delegation of blacks who had been involved with the Azusa Street outpourings to request use of Angelus Temple to hold a thirtieth anniversary celebration. Their request was granted, and in April of that year, the event, which Cotton depicted in the advertising flier as "a great getting together that we might be renewed in the old-time Spirit and power," was held. Saints from many parts of the world came to the temple for what was slated to be a week of celebration.

The anniversary meeting was considered an overwhelming spiritual success. Indeed, the meeting was so successful that it garnered letters and telegrams of interest and support from several countries. The projected week found the Cottons and their followers staying until October—a six-month event. During those six months, Elder and "Mother" Cotton joined other notable Pentecostal speakers to minister daily. In multiracial worship services reminiscent of harmony experienced at the old Azusa Street meetings, thousands were again drawn to the church. Many stayed for up to eighteen hours at a time to experience preaching, prayer, shouting, dancing in the spirit, and divine healing. One historian contends that the meetings came at a crucial time for Angelus Temple. They were just what the declining congregation needed to regain its prominence.[2] McPherson herself credited the meetings with being the launching pad that attracted renewed worldwide attention to the Pentecostal movement.[3]

But Emma Cotton holds the further distinction of being one of only a small number of Azusa Street participants—few of them women—to attempt to write an eyewitness, though somewhat problematic account of the revival. Her recounting of the event was contained in a single article entitled "The Inside Story of the Outpouring of the Holy Spirit—Azusa Street—April 1906." It appeared in the only extant volume of *Message of the Apostolic Faith,* a newsletter she personally published in April 1939, thirty years after the demise of the revivals heyday.

Her story appeared almost simultaneously and verbatim in the April 6, 1936, edition of the Assembly of God's periodical, *The Pentecostal Evangel* in an article entitled "When the Spirit Fell in Los Angeles." Cotton is not mentioned as the author, however. The attribution simply reads "an eye-witness account."

The short piece can be more correctly called a nostalgic recollection than a true eyewitness account. It focuses primarily on the events that unfolded at the Bonnie Brae prayer meeting before the revival moved to Azusa Street. But is it among the very few pieces of information we have about the revival from people who were actually there.

Cotton's report of the Azusa Street revival is short and apparently incomplete. Yet it is one of the few published accounts that historians repeatedly cite and to which they give credence. According to Cotton, at the time the article was written, she had in her possession much valuable information of the saints of God, including "extracts from the old and original papers published during the outpouring." She intended to use this information to publish sequels to the initial installment and told her readers that "I have much more to say about the wonderful working of the Power of God among the people next time, if the Lord wills."[4] Whether she did is not known since subsequent volumes of the newsletter cannot be accounted for.

Despite J. Douglas Nelson's[5] contention that Cotton's account is biased by her gender, she draws serious attention to the role women played in the revival. While most other accounts generally gave the prominent place to the leadership of men, Cotton was insistent that women such as Lucy Farrow and Hutchins were crucial to the unfolding and success of the revival. In her account, Cotton nostalgically reminisces:

> While I write this, my soul is lifted up because I saw the house in the first glory, and when I remember those days, I feel like going down to the dust in humility, if only to bring back the old-time power, I am ready to give my life.
> . . . The old-time Azusa work stood for and still stands for "the earnestly contending for the faith once delivered to the saints."[6]

McPherson had a great deal of respect for Cotton and encouraged her to establish the Azusa Pentecostal Temple in Los Angeles. Cotton co-pastored this church with her husband. Henry was probably still employed with the railroad, so Emma was considered the more prominent minister and did the bulk of the preaching for perhaps two reasons: First, his work schedule gave her the time and freedom to hone her preaching crafts though the numerous itinerant preaching engagements she accepted, and second, it also kept Henry away from the church when Emma had to take charge. The church remained an independent congregation throughout her lifetime, for although the Cottons were associated with the Church of God in Christ and probably held credentials with that organization, the denomination did not allow women to serve as pastors.

Today the church is known as the Crouch Memorial Pentecostal Church of God in Christ and is located at 1001 East 27th Street in East Los Angeles, California. The church is named for Samuel Crouch, one of Emma Cotton's protégés whom she encouraged and nurtured in the ministry while he was a young man. Crouch took over the pastorate of the church, went on to build it into a sizable congregation, and became a bishop in the Church of God in Christ. In 1945, Emma and Henry hosted the thirty-ninth anniversary of the Azusa Street Revival at the church that they pastored, though this was a much smaller celebration than was held nine years earlier.

Besides being a preacher, Emma Cotton was a songwriter. Some historians credit her with penning the popular black spiritual tune "When the Saints Go Marching In." The authorship of this piece, however, cannot be entirely corroborated. Yet another gospel favorite among early Pentecostals, "John Saw That Number," is also attributed and confirmed to have been penned by Cotton.

During the early days of the anniversary revival, Cotton spoke of the early Azusa Street meeting in a testimony reprinted in the April 29, 1936, issue of McPherson's *Foursquare Crusader:*

> God was exalted and the power fell. When the power fell, people left their big churches and temples and went to that old barn to pray. The lame, the halt and the blind came and God healed them. It was a common thing to have three or four messages from the

word in one meeting. The saints were so saturated with the power of God that the thing swept the city and oh, how the power fell.[7]

Cotton wrote in 1936, "In those days when they said God would heal you, you were healed. For thirty years, "I never have gone back to the doctor . . . nor any old medicine."[8] In 1950, after forty-four years of remission, Cotton's cancer recurred in an incurable form. She died of the disease in 1952 at the age of seventy-five and is buried in Lincoln Memorial Park in Compton, California. Henry died in 1959.

chapter 19

Rachel Harper Sizelove

WE KNOW MORE about Rachel Sizelove's life before coming to Azusa Street than any of the other women. For unlike so many of the others, Sizelove seemed to have had at least a small sense of the historic, spiritual significance of the events that were unfolding around her. Because of that, she sought to preserve at least a small picture of those events through her own writing and the preservation of the eyewitness accounts from *The Apostolic Faith*.

Rachel Harper's father fought for the Union in the American Civil War, and she was born a year before it ended. She was raised in Marengo, Indiana, a small prairie town bordering the Ohio River in the northeastern-central portion of the state, 115 miles south of Indianapolis and 36 miles west of Louisville, Kentucky. Her mother and grandmother were devout Methodists, and as a young girl, Rachel and her six brothers and sisters attended the Pilot Knob Sunday School.

From a young age, Rachel was interested in pursuing education. However, she had to forego formal training during long periods of her early life because of her mother's constant sickness and the family's meager resources. As a young child, she was required to pitch in to help care for the home and her siblings. As an adolescent, she was hired out for day work to help supplement the small income her father was able to provide as a lumberman and farmer.

But Rachel never lost her desire for an education. She saved as much as possible of the money she made from days working and pressed her father to allow her to pursue schooling as soon as it was convenient for the family. That day came when, as a young woman, Rachel attended the Teacher's Institute in Gordon, Indiana, to receive a teaching certificate.

The schoolmaster, Professor Johnson, was a United Brethren preacher and godly man who regularly called his students together for a time of prayer and Bible reading. He also invited other ministers to hold revival meetings on the campus. While studying at the institute, Rachel was converted in a union revival meeting held on the school grounds by two ministers: one a Free Methodist, the other United Brethren—both Holiness groups who held to the doctrine of entire sanctification.

In 1894, at the age of twenty and having obtained the teaching certificate, Rachel moved to Kansas where her sister Mary and her husband were living. Shortly after arriving in the community, Rachel passed the test for a teaching license and became the school marm in a one-room schoolhouse. Her students ranged from very young children to men and women at least her age. The young children attended regularly, while the older students came to school as the rigorous farming schedule allowed. Among them was Joseph Sizelove, a young farmer who was her oldest student. The two struck up a friendship that blossomed into strong affection.

Rachel planned to save money from her teaching job and go to Lebanon, Kansas, with her sister Florence to further her education. But her relationship with Joseph changed her intentions. Soon after Joseph was converted in a revival meeting they attended together, the two were married. When Rachel had been converted, she felt the Lord had laid it on her heart to "get sinners saved." Apparently Josie (as she affectionately called him) had felt a similar urging. Not long after he was saved, the couple began their involvement in the ministry serving as altar workers, praying with others who wanted to be converted.

Josie and Rachel soon moved to Edwards County, Kansas, to homestead federal government land. Not wanting to curtail their spiritual fervor in the somewhat isolated environment, the two started a Sunday school in their small dugout home that drew neighbors from the surrounding community. Obviously, others shared their need for spiritual edification; the Sizemores' class was so successful that people crowded in doors and windows to hear their instruction, and the town stopped its Sunday baseball game so that people could attend. Because of the success of this effort, Josie soon began itinerant preaching.

Life on the prairie involved constant deprivation. The Sizeloves had seven children, three of whom died as infants. They were challenged by drought and failed crops, meager provisions of food, makeshift housing, and constant travel. They also suffered periods of loneliness when they were apart so that Josie could find work or be a part of a protracted revival meeting.

Their early married life also involved constant moving since, even as ministers, they were subject to relocation as the need required. In the two years between 1892 and 1894, for example, the Sizelove family moved three times. In 1892, Rachel and Josie were appointed Free Methodist circuit riders for a territory that covered eastern Kansas and a large portion of Oklahoma. During the next three years, they traveled by wagon from town to town to such places as Arkansas City, Kansas; Ponca City and Enid, Oklahoma. They held their first gospel meeting in Fort Dodge, Kansas in 1893. Later that year they were appointed to a charge in Aragona, Kansas. They covered a circuit that extended down to the newly opened Oklahoma Territory. In 1894 they were appointed to set up new congregations for the Free Methodists in Oklahoma.

During much of this time, Rachel was either sick or nursing and nurturing her children. She traveled with Josie as often as possible, usually taking all of the children with her. When she was with him, she and Josie both preached and ministered in the meetings.

Throughout these years, one of Rachel's major concerns was that her children would receive an education. Life as a prairie circuit-riding family meant that the children received instruction in a very haphazard manner. In 1895, the Sizeloves came to Los Angeles so that their children could take advantage of the free education available through the Free Methodist Seminary. By the time of the Azusa Street Revival, eleven years later, Rachel and her family were still living in the Free Methodist colony, only a short distance from the mission's location in downtown Los Angeles.

When the Azusa Street Revival got underway, Rachel and Josie Sizelove had been circuit-riding evangelists involved for almost two decades in Holiness and revival circles. Much of the ecstatic worship of Azusa Street was similar to what they had experienced in the Holiness camp meetings they had conducted and attended across the Midwest. They were accustomed to exuberant demonstrations of God's Spirit and had seen prophetic declarations, divine healing, shouting, and being slain in the Spirit time and time again. So Rachel at first regarded the Azusa Street Revival only as a curiosity and showed little interest in attending the meetings. In fact, on first being told about the meeting, Sizelove declined to attend because she did not want to get involved in something fanatical, as the element of tongue-speaking might suggest. So by the time Sizelove finally decided to attend the Azusa Street meeting in June 1906, the revival had been underway for two months. What she observed there added a new dimension to all that she had previously. Sizelove describes her first encounter with the revival in this way:

> . . . I heard there was a company of people in an old building, speaking in tongues as on the day of Pentecost. My husband passed by and heard such wonderful singing in the Spirit . . . as we entered the old building; somehow, I was touched by the presence of God. It was such a humble place with its low ceilings and rough floors. Cobwebs were hanging in the windows and joists . . . The Lord had chosen this humble spot to gather all nationalities, to baptize them with the Holy Ghost. It was in the afternoon when I first went there. There were about twelve of God's children, white and colored, there tarrying before the Lord, some sitting and some kneeling. . . .
>
> My very soul cried out, "O! Lord, these people have something I do not have." Brother Seymour gave out the Word and made an altar call and said anyone who wanted to seek the Lord for pardon or sanctification or the Baptism of the Holy Ghost and fire to come and bow at the altar. I thought, "Well, praise God, he is not doing away with any of my experience or belief, but just adding to my experience that of the Baptism of the Holy Ghost, which he said would come to a clean heart.["]
>
> I went home and began to search the Word of God. I saw it was in the Bible. I was again in the mission in July, 1906. By that time the crowds were beginning to gather. When Brother Seymour gave the altar call, I with many went to the altar. Raising my hands toward heaven I said, "Lord, I want my inheritance, the Baptism of the Holy Ghost and fire." Instantly in the Spirit I saw as it were a bright star away in the distance and my very soul crying out to God . . . O, I knew it was He as He came nearer He was in the form of a white dove.[1]

As depicted in her testimony, soon after her first visit to the revival, Sizelove and Josie had their own Pentecostal experiences.

While apparently they played no major role in the revival itself, it is probable that they did little more than regularly add their testimony to those of the saints and pray at the altar with those seeking conversion or the baptism of the Holy Spirit. For Josie and Rachel had come to Azusa Street primarily seeking their own personal revival. So at first, just to be part of the congregation, to be able to praise God in a new tongue and give their testimonies with the other saints was enough for them. Yet the contribution Rachel Sizelove was to make to spread the Pentecostal movement throughout the Los Angeles area and the Midwest was just beginning.

Sizelove was one of the women licensed by the Azusa Street Mission when her Methodist church rejected what they considered to be the fanaticism of the Pentecostal movement, making her no longer able to serve as a Free Methodist circuit rider. During the revival, it was a regular occurrence that people were told through visions and prophecy where they should go to carry the message of Pentecostalism. Those who were obedient were overwhelmed by the results of their ministry wherever they went. Rachel Sizelove was one of those to experience and share such a vision in which "the Lord showed me that I must go back east and tell my mother and brothers and sisters what the Lord had done for me and bring them the blessed message."[2]

In the later part of May 1907, when Sizelove left to carry the message to Springfield, Missouri, a small group of Azusa Street saints gathered around her and, as usual, laid hands on her and prayed in tongues as they were accustomed to doing for many who left the meetings on their God-ordained missions. The Holy Spirit spoke by interpretation and simply said, "Go, and go quickly!"[3]

As she traveled by train to Springfield, Sizelove met "a dear colored sister" who had also been at Azusa Street and was on her way to the East Coast to embark by ship to Africa.[4] The two women found quick fellowship and joined together to "talk to everyone [they] could about the mighty outpouring of the Holy

Ghost and tell them Jesus was coming soon." The two got permission to conduct worship services on the train and, though
they did not report any conversions or any instance of reception
of the Pentecostal experience, people listened intently as they
preached and ministered.[5]

Once she arrived at Springfield, she held worship services at
her family's house and confined much of her early preaching in
the area to cottage prayer meetings. By the time she left, however, several people had received the Holy Spirit baptism with
tongues—her sister Lillian Corum being the first person to
receive the Pentecostal experience in Springfield. Several other
family members, including her nephews Fred and Jim, also were
baptized in the Holy Spirit with tongues.

As excitement and word of her ministry spread, the group
from Springfield was soon joined by a group from Joplin,
Missouri, some eighty miles southwest of Springfield. Together
they purchased a tent and began to hold meetings that often
drew large crowds. After several weeks, however, they returned
to holding cottage meetings.

Though Sizelove is generally noted for her work in Springfield,
she was also instrumental in setting the stage for a second event
in Los Angeles that was to have great impact on the early
Pentecostal movement. Sometime in 1907, Sizelove had a dream
of "many white tents pitched at Arroyo Seco at the foot of the
hills in Hermon," California, where she was living. Thinking
about what the dream might mean, she came to understand it as
God's leading to hold a camp meeting near the Free Methodist
enclave where she and her husband resided, "so that the Free
Methodist people could receive the Baptism of the Holy Spirit."
Sizelove then shared this dream and the interpretation of it with
Seymour and the leaders of the Azusa Street Mission, and after
prayerful consideration the Arroyo Seco camp meeting was
launched.[6] This initial meeting was not in itself particularly significant, but the establishment of the Arroyo Seco camp meeting
site set the stage for the 1913 worldwide camp meeting that was

pivotal for the Pentecostal movement.

The Arroyo Seco meeting ran concurrently with the then-dwindling Azusa Street meetings. It drew even larger crowds and world-famous speakers such as faith healer Maria Woodworth-Etter. Many future Pentecostal leaders such as Watson Ague and Garfield T. Haywood received their baptism at the meeting. It was also at this meeting that the controversial teaching concerning the correct baptism formula arose when Robert E. McAlister became the first person to preach the message of baptism "in Jesus' name." This controversy would soon grow into the same level major conflict as the earlier "finished work" issue, which divided Seymour from the followers of William Durham. It would split the Pentecostal movement for a second time in its short history. What started out as a simple attempt to make the Pentecostal message accessible to the Free Methodists would result in one of the major schisms of the Pentecostal movement.

Sizelove returned to Springfield that same year for an extended time of ministry. Though on the earlier trip she had come alone, on this second trip Rachel was accompanied by Josie. The two stayed in the city for several months and preached wherever they were invited. It was during this visit that she had a vision of a "sparkling fountain springing up out of Springfield": "There appeared before me a beautiful, bubbling, sparkling fountain in the heart of the city of Springfield. It sprang up gradually but irresistibly and began to flow toward the East and toward the West, toward the North and toward the South, until the whole land was deluged in water."[7]

In November 1913, Rachel formally organized the little congregation that had formed around her preaching and placed Lillian, her sister, as pastor of the first Assemblies of God congregation in Springfield. It later became Central Assembly of God—a thriving congregation and church that would play a significant role in the denomination's history. It was the in the basement of this church that the Central Bible College, the first Assemblies of God institution of higher education, began in 1922.

By May 1918, the Assemblies of God had established its first headquarters in Findlay, Ohio, and moved it to St. Louis, Missouri. However, the denomination set up its Bible Publishing House in Springfield, and several Assemblies of God staffers moved to the city to support it. The publishing house was next joined by the Bible College and eventually the Assemblies of God moved its headquarters to the city.

Whether she sensed the true historic importance of the events that were unfolding around her at that time may be questioned. In 1925, Sizelove wrote a two-hundred-page autobiography, "Sketch of My Life." Interestingly, she did not hold either the Azusa Street Revival or her vision of Springfield and its subsequent unfolding as centrally important to her own spiritual journey. Rather, she apparently saw them as one of the many ways in which that journey had unfolded. She devoted only six pages to the Azusa Street Revival and does not mention the Springfield vision. Yet hers is one of the few extant eyewitness accounts and one of even fewer accounts of the Azusa Street Revival by women. She left the Springfield vision to others for interpretation and the attachment of significance. Several historians of the Assemblies of God do just that.

By 1934, however, Sizelove seemed to have a deeper appreciation of the historic import of all that had occurred in her life and submitted her story of the Springfield vision to *Word and Work,* the Pentecostal newsletter that her nephew Fred Corum and L. W. Bakewell were publishing in Framingham, Massachusetts. The first installment of her story appeared on the front page of the June issue. The March 1935 issue carried a second installment. The May 1939 issue of the newsletter carried an article by Sizelove entitled "The Temple" in which she again recounts the early days of the Azusa revival and likens the glory of those meetings to the Old Testament Shekinah glory that filled Solomon's Temple. In addition, the newsletter carried at least two other articles about Sizelove during that period. Mrs. J. J. Corum, Rachel's niece, wrote "A Sparkling Fountain: How a

Handmaiden of the Lord Kept the Army in Rank" for the July 1934 issue. An article entitled "Azusa's First Camp-Meeting" in the January 1936 issue was simply credited to the editors.

Sizelove died in 1941 in Long Beach, California, at the age of seventy-seven. Seven years before her death, she made an invaluable contribution to the unfolding legacy of the Azusa Street Revival. Her sense of history prompted her to collect and save the individual issues of *The Apostolic Faith*. In a 1924 letter to her nephews, James and Fred Corum, Sizelove explains her motivation for donating her material for publication:

> Mr. Jim and Fred Corum:
> My dear brother and nephew, I am sending you by mail a copy of all of the papers printed at the Azusa Street Mission, which was only thirteen, for before the fourteenth paper was published, Sister Crawford ventured out from the Azusa publishing house and set up in Portland, Oregon. I am sending the first and second papers that she printed in Portland . . . I believe the dear Lord will get glory out of the reprinting of the papers in book form, for so many Saints say they would like so much to read the old papers.
> . . . I do not know of anyone who has the picture of Brother Seymour and Brother Smith his co-worker, who had been an old Methodist preacher for years and so well-known and loved by all who knew him. I would like their pictures taken just from their waist up and I think they could be taken from the group picture. They are both in glory now. I think it would be nice to have a picture of the letterhead they used in the beginning of Pentecost, to be printed just above the picture of the Azusa St. Mission, for God did get glory out of those letters. For, when so many just saw the top of the letter, conviction would seize them for their baptism, and the power of God would fall upon them, Hallelujah!
> Now dear ones if you can take these papers . . . print a book to the glory of God, I will be so glad to donate my share of any revenues to the Bethel Home there in Framingham. I would like to donate some money to help get it printed if Josie is willing. But

I am praying that God will furnish the means that it will be printed and I will do all in my power by the help of God to sell the
book and the proceeds go to Bethel Home as long as you are in
charge. . . . So pray over it. Wait upon God. It may be that He
will raise someone up to help print the book. I do not want one
cent out of the book to spend upon myself. I want, for my part,
to donate every cent to the cause. Look these papers over and see
what can be done, and if you decide you can print it, do as you
are led of the Lord with your part of any proceeds.

I enjoy reading the Word and Work so much. I am sending a
small contribution to help with it.

With love and prayers, I am your old aunt,

Rachel Sizelove[8]

Every historian of Pentecostalism is indebted to Sizelove for
this one singular act. Her understanding of the importance of
education possibly fueled her understanding of the need for
sources to study. In any case, her foresight and generosity have
preserved a wealth that just now is being completely mined.

Conclusion

WASHERWOMEN, HOUSEMAIDS, TEACHERS, PREACHERS— they all came to one place for the spiritual experience of their lifetimes, bringing with them a breadth of social, cultural, and spiritual diversity. For much of the one hundred years since Azusa Street they have remained unnamed, misnamed, or simply footnotes to the dynamic history of the movement.

The women of Azusa Street exemplify the racial and economic diversity of the Azusa Street Revival in a time in American history that was heavily stratified along those lines. White women—Florence Crawford, Clara Lum, Lucy Leatherman, Lillian Garr, Ivey Campbell, Rachel Sizelove, Ardella Mead, May Evans, Mabel Smith Witter Hall, Anna Hall, and Daisy Batman worked alongside black women—Neely Terry, Lucy Farrow, Julia Hutchins, Ophelia Wiley, Jennie Evans Seymour, and Emma Cotton—joining Latino women—Susie Valdez and Rosa de Lopez.

This was no women's rights movement, and they gave no attention to that larger issue. It was not their concern. Rather, they played out a practical feminism in sharing with their brethren the singular understanding that Jesus was soon to return; what they, as well as their brethren, were called to do, they must do quickly and with all their heart. They focused their attention on being equally involved in winning the lost and bringing a full measure of the kingdom into the personal reality of the lives they touched.

They came looking for power and found it. Power to speak in unknown and known tongues. Power to preach the gospel with conviction. Power for healing and deliverance. Power to withstand the rigors of ministry and the assaults of the mockers and scorners.

They came looking for a place to serve the God they loved. Looking for a place where they, as women fully qualified by the Spirit, could function without restraint alongside their male colleagues. For the most part, they found it in the revival itself, and in congregations they touched within the small towns and large cities of America and on mission fields throughout the world. Everywhere they went they told and retold their stories through tongues and interpretation, in their native languages, through testimonies, sermon, and song. And through the undeniable truth and power of their witness, people were challenged to accept the validity of the Pentecostal experience.

Their stories have been gleaned from a variety of primary and secondary resources: newspaper articles in the religious and secular press, "eyewitness" accounting of the revival—most of them written by men, and many of them written several years after the revival's demise or handed down to second ears by oral tradition before being committed to paper. They are from personal correspondences to Holiness and Pentecostal colleagues all over the world as well as camp meeting and revival fliers and posters.

Many sources only mention these women in passing, giving them a sentence or a paragraph here or there. But when woven together, they create a template for a rich tapestry that more fully discloses the story of the early Pentecostal revival at Azusa Street, its forerunner, the Bonnie Brae Street prayer meeting, and the even earlier revivals in Kansas and Houston under Charles Parham.

In part, we can assess the impact of these women's lives and ministries by looking at the ministries of the men and women they nurtured in the faith, the churches they helped build, and the denominations they formed or influenced. As wives, mothers, pastors, and visionaries, they led men to faith. The impartation of the Pentecostal experience came through their hands, and they worked alongside their male colleagues to energize the fledgling movement and spread its message around the world.

Several women were part of the important linkages that positioned William Seymour at the head of the revival. A woman introduced him to the doctrine of initial evidence, the experience of speaking in tongues, and the progenitor of both. A woman pastor issued the invitation that brought him to Los Angeles, and another woman's suggestion prompted that decision. Along with the unfortunate treatment he later received at the hands of some of his white brethren, Seymour felt betrayed by two women—Crawford and Lum, who left the ministry taking with them the mailing list—its financial mainstay and link to its supporters and followers around the world. Even before coming to Azusa Street, a number of the women had worked with some of the most powerful leaders and future leaders of the movement. Several had worked with Parham. Leatherman and Lum had been part of Charles Hanley's World's Faith Missionary Association. Ardella Mead and her husband worked with Methodist missionary pioneer William Taylor. Others were to encounter and work with prominent leaders after leaving the revival. Cotton was an associate of Aimee Semple McPherson. Mabel Smith and Jennie Evans Seymour preached for William Durham in Chicago.

They were influential in the lives of male colleagues who were later to assume prominence. Leatherman invited Thomas Ball Barratt, the Norwegian Pentecostal leader, to a revival meeting and later prayed with him to receive the Holy Spirit baptism with tongues. Lucy Farrow was esteemed by many in the movement, but perhaps none more than Howard Goss, the future oneness leader. Susie Valdez's son, A. C. Valdez, Sr., became an important leader in the Assemblies of God. Ivy Campbell was closely associated with Levi Lupton. Emma Cotton had substantial influence on the life and ministry of Samuel Crouch, a future bishop in the Church of God in Christ.

Their travels took them all over the world, and their collective ministry carried the Pentecostal message to five of the earth's seven continents. Many were pioneers in areas to which they felt called, traveling alone, with their husbands, or with teams of other missionaries. They endured the rigors of missionary life, the violence of mobs, and the derision of their families and organized religious bodies, all for the sake of the gospel.

Belief in and practice of divine healing was at the center of the early Pentecostal movement, and these women embraced this doctrine wholeheartedly. Miracles were wrought at their hands—the blind received sight, the lame walked, tumors fell off. Many who came to Azusa Street received physical healing along with their Spirit baptism. Florence Crawford was healed from a variety of chronic conditions, as were Clara Lum and Emma Cotton. Yet, in some cases, they themselves or close family members were to prematurely succumb to some of the same illnesses for which they had brought healing to others. Lillian Garr lost two children and died from complications of surgery at age thirty-eight. Ivy Campbell died of an undisclosed condition at age forty-four. The entire Evans family perished while serving as missionaries in Africa.

Certainly, there were other women strategically involved in the ministry of the Azusa Street Mission and Revival. Phoebe Sargent and Sister Prince were two of the twelve members of the administrative board at the Azusa Street Mission, but we have no more information on them than their names with a notation that Sargent was appointed a city evangelist along with Seymour's soon-to-be wife, Jennie Evans Moore, and Prince was described as "A Mother in Israel."[1] Louisa Condit went with Lucy Leatherman to Palestine. Myrtle Shideler accompanied her husband and the Meads to Angola. Leila McKinney accompanied her aunt, Pastor Julia Hutchins, to Liberia.

For the most part, these women held no denominational positions. The bulk of these women were either itinerant evangelists or missionaries. They lived the "faith life," depending on offerings from their more-or-less frequent preaching engagements to sustain their livelihood. Only Hutchins and Farrow were pastors of small congregations, though Garr and Sizelove served alongside their husbands as heads of congregations from time to time. Only one woman, Florence Crawford, led a denomination which in comparison to many other Pentecostal bodies remains numerically small, though its geographical reach extends around the world. Rachel Sizelove had a vision that is credited for pinpointing God's perfect location for the headquarters of another denomination.

The Azusa Street Revival lasted eight years. By its end in 1914, there were more than twenty denominations and several hundred congregations in the United States that identified themselves as Pentecostal. In the twenty years following its close, several more denominations and several thousand congregations in the United States had been established, and several hundred more existing congregations had switched to the Pentecostal camp. By that time, the Pentecostal message had been heard all over the world. Women as well as men communicated the message and helped establish and build up these congregations and denominations.

It is not surprising that we know little of the women's participation in the Azusa Street Revival. In many instances, we know little of the men's participation. While some eyewitness reports pay some attention to individuals within these meetings, the participants themselves generally spoke in the third person, eschewing the identification of the specific deeds on any one person, preferring to see all accomplishments as solely the providential work of the Holy Spirit.

Summarizing the effects of the egalitarian understanding fostered in the ministry of women in the Pentecostal movement, an editor of an early Pentecostal periodical wrote:

Obscure men and women, boys and girls, have received from God definite calls. . . . A marked feature of this "latter day" outpouring is the Apostolate of women. . . . They did not push themselves to the front, God pulled them. They did not take this ministry on themselves, God put it on them.[2]

Even then, however, when you compare the accomplishments of the women of the Azusa Street Revival to those of their male colleagues, these women may at first seem to be only secondary players, their accomplishments insignificant. Yet, they were not bystanders or merely supporters. Their lives, work, and own words portray a level of commitment and involvement in every facet of ministry, despite restrictions that had found their way into the Pentecostal movement in its earliest stages. Indeed, a serious look at women's involvement with the revival, such as presented here, leads one to conclude that the impact of what occurred at the Azusa Street Revival, and in early Pentecostalism itself, would have been greatly reduced had women not been involved.

Much still remains to be told about their stories, which have been buried with the women for nearly one hundred years. This work, hopefully, will be a catalyst to spur interest in giving them the recognition they deserve. As more primary sources are unearthed, and we learn more about their personal and family lives, their education, and their early spiritual journeys, we will have a fuller portrait of what sparked the thirst of other women and men for the spiritual encounter that found itself in full flame at Azusa Street.

Notes

Introduction

1. Untitled article, *Message of The Apostolic Faith* 1, no. 10 (1907): 1.

2. Rachel Sizelove, "A Sparkling Fountain for the Whole Earth," *Word and Work* 56, no. 6 (June 1934).

3. For example, Julia Hutchins name is variably spelled Hutchinson, Rachel Sizelove is sometimes referred to as Sizemore, and Ardel Meade is Ardella in some references. I have found this true in many materials dealing with early evangelical religious movements. It signals, among other things, the lack of status women enjoyed as individuals even if they were full participants in the ministry.

Chapter One: Neely Terry

1. Ethel A. Goss, *The Winds of God* (New York: Comet Press Books, 1958), 70. Charles Parham ran the Bible school.

2. V. Alex Bills, "The Houston Connection: After Topeka and before Azusa Street." Paper presented at the 30th annual meeting of the Society for Pentecostal Studies, Kirkland, Wash., March 16–18, 2000.

3. James Tinney, "The Life of William Seymour," in Randall Burkett and Richard Newman, *Black Apostles: African American Clergy Confront the 20th Century* (Boston: G. K. Hall, 1978), 218.

Chapter Two: Julia Hutchins

1. "Testimonies of Outgoing Missionaries," *Apostolic Faith* 1, no. 2 (October 1906): 1.

2. Ibid.

3. Untitled article, *Apostolic Faith* 1, no. 4 (December 1906): 1.

4. Ibid.

5. "Sister Hutchins Testimony," *Apostolic Faith* 1, no. 2 (October 1906): 1.

6. "A Girl's Consecration for Africa," *Apostolic Faith* 1, no. 2 (October 1906): 1.

7. "Speeding to Foreign Lands," *Apostolic Faith* 1, no. 5 (January 1907): 3.

8. "In Africa," *Apostolic Faith* 1, no. 7 (April 1907): 1.

Chapter Three:
Lucy Farrow

1. Grant Wacker, *Heaven Below: Early Pentecostals and American Culture* (Cambridge, Mass.: Harvard University Press, 2001), 159.

2. Robert Longman, Jr., "Pre-Pentecostalist History." Spirithome.com: Resource for Spirituality and Faith. http://www.spirithome.com/hist-pent.html

3. Bills, "Houston Connection," 20.

4. Though several secondary sources report this, I found no original documentation of this as a fact.

5. Bills, "Houston Connection," 19.

6. Robert Owens, *Speak to the Rock—the Azusa Street Revival: Its Roots and Its Message* (Lanham, Md.: University Press of America, 2001).

7. Emma Cotton, "The Inside Story of the Outpouring of the Holy Spirit—Azusa Street, April 1906," *Apostolic Faith* 1, no. 1 (April 1936): 1–3.

8. "Pentecostal Experience," *Apostolic Faith* 1, no. 3 (November 1906): 4.

9. Farrow's and Seymour's early relationship is detailed by Susan Hyatt, "Spirit Filled Women," in *The Century of the Holy Spirit: 100 Years of Pentecostal and Charismatic Renewal* by Vinson Synan (Nashville, Tenn.: Thomas Nelson Publishers, 2001), 245–46.

10. Seymour was not actually admitted to the all-white classes but was allowed to sit outside the door

of the classroom to listen to Parham's lecture.

11. Untitled article, *Apostolic Faith* 1, no. 1 (September 1906): 1.

12. Cotton, "The Inside Story of the Outpouring," 2.

13. Frank Ewart, *The Phenomenon of Pentecost* (Hazelwood, Mo.: World Aflame Press, 1947), 74–76.

14. Ibid.

15. Paul Harvey, "Racism, Biracialism, and Interracialism in the Southern Religious Experience," in *Freedom's Coming: Religion, Race, and Culture in the South, 1860–2000* (City: University of California Press, 2005).

16. Goss, Winds of God, 56.

17. William Faupel, *The Everlasting Gospel: The Significance of Eschatology in the Development of Pentacostal Thought* (Sheffield, England: Sheffield Academic Press, 1996), 220.

18. Lucy Farrow, "The Work in Virginia," *Apostolic Faith* 1, no. 2 (October 1906): 3.

19. *Apostolic Faith* 1, no. 4 (December 1906): 1.

20. Ibid.

21. *Apostolic Faith* 1, no. 12 (September 1907): 1.

22. Ibid.

Chapter Four:
Clara Lum

1. Clara Lum, "Pentecostal Testimonies," *Apostolic Faith* 1, no. 6 (February 1907): 4.

2. Edith Blumhofer, "Clara E. Lum," in *Assemblies of God Heritage* 21 (Summer 2001): 17.

3. Ibid.

4. "Miss Clara Lum Writes Wonders," *Missionary World* (August 1906): 2.

5. Lum, "Pentecostal Testimonies," 4.

6. Ibid.

7. Clara Lum to T. B. Barratt, University of Oslo Archives, T. B. Barratt Etterlatte Papirer, MS 4ᵗ 33412, Daghalter, IX, 53, cited in David Bundy, "Spiritual Advice to a Seeker: Letters to T. B. Barratt from Azusa Street, 1906," *Pneuma* 14 (Fall 1992): 166.

8. Blumhofer, "Clara E. Lum," 18.

9. "Miss Clara Lum Writes Wonders," 2.

10. Edith M. Blumhofer and Grant Wacker, "Who Edited the Azusa Street Mission's *Apostolic Faith*?" in *Assemblies of God Heritage* 21 (Summer 2001): 17.

11. Ithiel Clemmons, *Bishop C. H. Mason and the Roots of the Church of God in Christ* (Bakersfield, Calif.: Pneuma Life Publications, 1996), 50.

12. "Manifestations Continue, Many Different Experiences. The Los Angeles Mission Reports through Miss Clara E. Lum," *Missionary World* (August 1906): 8.

13. "Gracious Pentecostal Showers Continue to Fall," *Apostolic Faith* 1, no. 3 (November 1906): 1.

14. "Clara Lum" in *New Dictionary of Pentecostal and Charismatic Movements* (Grand Rapids, Mich: Zondervan Publishing House, 2002), 561.

15. Blumhofer & Wacker, "Who Edited the Azusa Street," 19.

16. Ibid.

Chapter 5: Florence Reed Crawford

1. Florence Crawford, *The Light of Life Brought Triumph: A Brief Sketch of the Life and Labors of Florence L (Mother) Crawford.* Commemorative Edition. (Portland, Ore.: *Apostolic Faith* Publishing House, 1955), 3–4.

2. Ibid., 9.

3. Ibid.

4. "The Faith Way," *Apostolic Faith* 1, no. 3 (November 1906): 3.

5. Untitled article, *Apostolic Faith* 1, no. 2 (October 1906): 1.

6. Ibid.

7. Untitled article, *Apostolic Faith* 1, no. 5 (January 1907): 4.

8. "Color Line Obliterated," in *The (Portland) Morning Oregonian,* December 31, 1906, 9. Little is reported about Mildred after those early years, but there is evidence that she remained active in the church that her mother founded. It is known that Mildred collaborated with Raymond in writing several hymns.

9. "San Francisco and Oakland," *Apostolic Faith* 1, no. 4 (December 1906): 4.

10. Cecil M. Robeck, "Florence Crawford: *Apostolic Faith* Pioneer," in Grant Wacker and James Goff, *Portraits of a Generation* (Fayetteville: University of Arkansas Press, 2002), 229.

11. *Doctrines and Disciplines of the Azusa Street Mission of Los Angeles California,* ed. Larry Martin, vol. 7 of *The Complete Azusa Street Library* (Joplin, Mo.: Christian Life Books, 2000).

12. Ibid.

13. Quoted in J. C. Vanzandt, *Speaking in Tongues* (Portland, Ore.: Vanzandt Publications, 1926), 37.

14. "Camp Meeting: Apostolic Faith," *Time* magazine (August 19, 1935), 34–35.

15. For more on this schism see Robert E. Mitchell, *Heritage and Horizons: The History of the Open Bible Standard Churches* (Des Moines, Iowa: Open Bible Standard Churches, 1982).

16. Ibid., xv.

Chapter Six:
Lucy Leatherman

1. Robert M. Anderson, *Vision of the Disinherited: The Making of American Pentecostalism* (Peabody, Mass.: Hendrickson Publications, 1979), 130–31.

2. Untitled article, *Apostolic Faith* 1, no. 4 (December 1906): 1.

3. "Fear Witchcraft, Mob Missionaries," *Des Moines Capitol*, August 7, 1907, 3.

4. "Pentecostal Experience," *Apostolic Faith* 1, no. 3 (November 1906): 4.

5. Lucy Leatherman, "A Missionary Trip Through Syria and Palestine," *The Pentecost*, December 1, 1908, 15.

6. Lucy Leatherman, "Apostolic Revival in Egypt," *The Pentecost*, January–February 1909, 5.

7. "Jerusalem," *Apostolic Faith* 1, no. 13 (May 1907).

8. Lucy Leatherman, "Coming Home," *The Pentecost*, September 15, 1909, 4.

9. Ibid.

10. Lucy Leatherman, "Brief notes: The Philippines," *Confidence*,

February 15, 1910, 15.

11. "News from Miss Lucy Leatherman," *Confidence*, August 1912, 185.

12. Charles Conn, *Where the Saints have Trod* (Cleveland, Tenn.: Pathway Press, 1959), 18.

Chapter Seven:
Ophelia Wiley

1. "Healed Blind Woman," Salem (Oregon) *Daily Capitol Journal*, December 24, 1906, 6.

2. "Meeting Closes Early," Salem (Oregon) *Daily Capitol Journal*, December 28, 1906, 7.

3. Brother Ryan Receives His Pentecost, *Apostolic Faith* 1, no. 3 (November 1906): 3.

4. Larry Martin, *The Life and Ministry of William J. Seymour*, vol. 1 of *The Complete Azusa Street Library* (Joplin, Mo.: Christian Life Books, 1999), 239.

5. "Holy Rollers Had it Bad," *Los Angeles Times*, August 14, 1906, 114.

6. "Ask What Ye Will," *Apostolic Faith* 1, no. 2 (October 1906): 3.

7. "Sermon from a Dress," *Apostolic Faith* 1, no. 2 (October 1906): 2.

8. "In The Upper Room," *Apostolic Faith* 1, no. 4 (December 1906): 4.

9. See for example, "New Tongues Movement," *Salem Daily Oregon Statesman*, November 20, 1906, 2; "Claim Gift of Tongues," *Dallas (Oregon) Polk County Observer*, December 28, 1906, 1; and "Healed Blind Woman," *Salem (Oregon) Daily Capitol Journal*,

December 24, 1906, 6.
  10. "Meeting Closes Early," 6.
  11. Martin, *Life and Ministry of Seymour*, 230.

Chapter Eight: Lillian Anderson Garr

  1. Ewart, *Phenomenon of Pentecost*, 179.
  2. "Good News From Danville, Virginia," *Apostolic Faith* 1, no. 1 (September 1906): 4.
  3. "Pentecost in Danville, Va.," *Apostolic Faith* 1, no. 2 (October 1906): 2.
  4. "Good News From Danville," 4.
  5. "Pentecost in Danville," 2.
  6. Grant Wacker, *Heaven Below: Early Pentecostals and American Culture* (Cambridge, Mass.: Harvard University Press, 2001), 50.
  7. Alfred Garr and Lillian Garr, "The Work in India," *Apostolic Faith* 11, no. 9 (June 1907): 4.
  8. "Testimony and Praise to God," *Apostolic Faith* 1, no. 9 (June 1907): 4.
  9. Stanley Frodsham, "A Wonderful Life Ended," *Confidence* 5, no. 9 (May 1916): 80.
  10. Ibid., 79.

Chapter Nine: Susie Villa Valdez

  1. Valdez, *Fire on Azusa Street*, 23.
  2. Thomas R. Nickel, *Azusa Street Outpouring: As Told to Me by Those who Were There* (Hanford, Calif.: Great Commission International, 1979), 12.
  3. Valdez, *Fire on Azusa Street*, 41–42. This meeting is a crucial turning point in the Pentecostal movement and is the place where one of the first major schisms, the split over the oneness doctrine of the necessity for the baptism "in Jesus' name," had its roots.
  4. Ibid., 2.
  5. Ibid., 3–4.
  6. Ibid., 106–7.

Chapter Ten: Rosa de Lopez

  1. "Spanish Receive Pentecost," *Apostolic Faith* 1, no. 2 (October 1906): 4
  2. Camillo Alverez, "Hispanic Pentecostals: Azusa Street and Beyond," *Encounter* 63, nos. 1–2(Winter 2002): 13.
  3. "Spanish Receive Pentecost," 4.
  4. "Bible Pentecost" *Apostolic Faith* 1, no. 3 (November 1906): 1
  5. "Preaching to The Spanish," *Apostolic Faith* (November 1906): 4.
  6. Gaston Espinosa, "The Silent Pentecostals," *Christian History*, Issue 58, 17:2 (1998): 23.
  7. "Spanish Receive Pentecost," 4.
  8. Maria Woodworth-Etta, *Diary of Signs and Wonders* (Tulsa, Okla.: Harrison House, 1919), 450.
  9. "Gracious Pentecostal Showers Continue to Fall," *Apostolic Faith* 1, no. 3 (November 1906): 1.

Chapter Eleven: Ardella Knapp Mead

  1. William Taylor, *A Flaming Torch in Darkest Africa* (New York: Eaton and Mains, 1898), 485.
  2. "Sister Mead's Baptism," *Apostolic Faith* 1, no. 2 (November 1906): 3.

3. Ibid.
4. Untitled article, *Apostolic Faith*
1, no. 3 (October 1906): 3.
5. "A Message Concerning His
Coming," *Apostolic Faith* 1, no. 2
(October 1906): 3.
6. "Bro. Mead's Testimony of
Pentecost," *Apostolic Faith* 1, no. 3
(November 1906): 3.
7. "New-Tongued Missionaries,"
Apostolic Faith 1, no. 3 (November
1906): 2.
8. "Pentecost in New
York,"*Apostolic Faith* 1, no. 4
(December 1906): 4.
9. "Received Her Pentecost,"
Apostolic Faith 1, no. 5 (January
1907): 3.

Chapter Twelve:
Daisy Batman

1. Untitled article, *Apostolic Faith*
(October 1906): 4.
2. "Bro. G. W. Batman's
Testimony," *Apostolic Faith* 1, no. 4
(December 1906): 4.
3. "En Route to Africa,"
Apostolic Faith (December 1906): 4.
4. "Mrs. Daisy Batman's
Testimony," *Apostolic Faith* 1, no. 4
(December 1906): 4.
5. "En Route to Africa," 4
6. Ibid.

Chapter Thirteen:
May Evans

1. "The Same Old Way,"
Apostolic Faith 1, no. 1 (September
1906): 1.
2. Ibid.
3. "Testimony of Healing,"
Apostolic Faith 1, no. 3 (November
1906): 3.

4. Ibid.
5. Ibid.
6. "Fire Falling in Oakland,"
Apostolic Faith 1, no. 1 (September
1906): 4.
7. "Bro. Rosa's Testimony,"
Apostolic Faith 1, no. 1 (October
1906): 1.
8. "Spreading the Full
Gospel,"*Apostolic Faith* 1, no. 3
(November 1906): 1.
9. "Pentecost in Woodland,"
Apostolic Faith 1, no. 4 (December
1906), 1.

Chapter 14:
Anna Hall

1. "Jesus Is Coming," *Apostolic
Faith* 1, no. 1 (September 1906): 4.
2. Zion, Illinois, was the home of
faith healer John Alexander Dowie's
Christian Catholic Apostolic Church
and utopian community, which bore
the name "Shiloh."
3. Sarah Parham, *The Life of
Charles Fox Parham: Founder of the
Apostolic Faith Movement* (New
York: Garland Publishing, 1985),
108.
4. Henry G. Tuthill, "History of
the Latter Rain," *The Faithful
Standard,* July 1922.
5. James Goff, *Fields White unto
Harvest: Charles F. Parham and the
Missionary Origins of Pentecostalism*
(Fayetteville: University of Arkansas
Press, 1988), 119.
6. "Jesus is Coming," 4.
7. "Russians Hear in Their Own
Tongue, *Apostolic Faith* 1, no. 1
(September 1906): 4.
8. "The Polishing Process,"
Apostolic Faith 1, no. 2 (October
1906): 4.

9. "Honor the Holy Ghost," *Apostolic Faith* 1, no. 2 (October 1906): 4.

10. *Apostolic Faith* (April 1925): 14. Cited in Bills, "Houston Connection."

Chapter Fifteen: Mabel Witter Smith Hall

1. Letter from Mabel Smith to Millicent McClendon and Howard Goss, February 25, 1907.

2. Frodsham, *With Signs Following*, 41.

3. G. J. Buck, *The Free Christian: What and Where is the Christian Religion?* (Waco, Tex: Hill, Kellner, Frost, 1906), 510.

4. Tuthill, "History of the Latter Rain," 8.

5. Parham, *The Life of Charles F. Parham* (New York: Garland Publishing Company, 1985), 145.

6. Goss, *Winds of God*, 91–92.

7. B. C. Lee, "When God Breathed on Zion," in Gordon P. Gardiner, *Out Of Zion: Into All The World* (Shippensburg, Pa.: Companion Press, 1990).

8. Dowie had organized the Christian Catholic Church in 1895 and formed the community of Zio City north of Chicago in 1900. His group practiced communal living and faith healing.

9. Letter from Mabel Smith to Millicent McClendon and Howard Goss, February 25, 1907.

10. Bills, "Houston Connection."

11. Tuthill, "History of the Latter Rain," 8.

Chapter Sixteen: Ivy Glenshaw Campbell

1. Pearl Bowen, "Akron Visited with Pentecost," *Apostolic Faith* 1, no. 5 (January 1907): 1.

2. "Report From Ohio and Pennsylvania," *Apostolic Faith* 1, no. 6 (February 1907): 4.

3. All these were carried under one title, "Pentecost in Middle States," *Apostolic Faith* 1, no. 6 (February 1907): 3.

4. "Demons Cast Out," *Apostolic Faith* 1, no. 6 (February 1907): 3.

5. Untitled article, *Apostolic Faith* 1, no. 6 (February 1907): 1.

6. Frank Bartleman, *How Pentecost Came to Los Angeles* (Los Angeles, Calif.: F. Bartleman, 1925), 43–48, 100.

7. "Tongues Gift Denounced," *Los Angeles Times*, January 7, 1907, 13.

8. Cecil M. Robeck, Jr., "Ivey Campbell and the Ohio Revival," unpublished manuscript, 24.

9. Ibid., 30.

10. Ibid., 25.

Chapter Seventeen: Jennie Evans Moore Seymour

1. "At Los Angeles, California," *Confidence*, October 1912, 232.

2. Jennie Evans Moore, "Music From Heaven," *Apostolic Faith* 1, no. 8 (May 1907): 3.

3. Ibid.

4. "At Los Angeles," 233–34.

5. Thomas R. Nickel, *In Those Days* (Monterey Park, Calif.: Great Commission International, 1962), 4.

6. Moore, "Music from Heaven," 3.

7. Untitled article, *Apostolic Faith* 12 (January 1908): 1.

8. "Bible Teaching on Marriage and Divorce," *Apostolic Faith* 1, no. 5 (January 1907): 3.

9. "The Marriage Tie," *Apostolic Faith* 1, no. 10 (September 1907): 3.

10. Durham insisted that salvation and Holy Spirit baptism involved a two-stage process and that sanctification was progressive. Seymour held the Wesleyan Holiness understanding that salvation and sanctification were two instantaneous experiences which would be followed by baptism in the Holy Spirit.

11. Martin, *Life and Ministry of William Seymour*, 331.

Chapter Eighteen: Emma Cotton

1. Cotton, "Inside Story," 1.

2. Daniel Mark Epstein, *Sister Aimee: The Life of Aimee Semple McPherson* (New York: Harcourt Brace Jovanovich, 1993), 405.

3. Aimee Semple McPherson, *This is That: Personal Experiences, Sermons and Writings of Aimee Semple McPherson* (The Bridal Call Publishing House, 1921), 45–47.

4. Cotton, "Inside Story," 3.

5. J. Douglas Nelson's Ph.D. dissertation, "For Such a Time as This," was the first work to take a serious look at the leadership of Seymour in the early Pentecostal movement.

6. Cotton, "Inside Story," 3.

7. "Divine Visitation at Temple like at Old Azusa Mission," *Foursquare Crusader* 2, no. 45 (April 29, 1936): 1.

8. Cotton, "Inside Story," 3.

Chapter Nineteen: Rachel Harper Sizelove

1. Rachel Sizelove,"A Sketch of My Life," unpublished manuscript, 196.

2. Rachel Sizelove, "A Sparkling Fountain for the Whole Earth," *Word and Work* 56, no. 6 (June 1934): 12.

3. Adapted from *Word and Work* 57, no. 3 (March 1935): 2.

4. It may have been Farrow or Hutchins or one of their party, though Sizelove does not provide specific information on who she was.

5. Sizelove, "Sparkling Fountain,"12.

6. "Azusa's First Camp-Meeting," *Word and Work* 58, no. 1 (January 1936): 1.

7. Sizelove, "Sparkling Fountain," 12.

8. Fred Corum, preface in *"Like as of Fire: Newspapers from the Azusa Street World Wide Revival* (Washington, D.C.: Mid Atlantic Regional Press, 1988).

Conclusion

1. Fred Corum, preface in *Like as of Fire.*

2. *The Weekly Evangel* 1, no.31 (March 18, 1916): 6.

Bibliography

Anderson, Robert Mapes. *Vision of the Disinherited: The Making of American Pentecostalism*. Peabody, Mass.: Hendrickson Publications, 1979.

Apostolic Faith Mission. *A Great Religious Leader: A Brief Sketch of the Life and Labors of Florence L. (Mother) Crawford, Founder of The Apostolic Faith Mission*. Portland, Ore.: Apostolic Faith Publishing House, 1965.

———. *An Historical Account of the Apostolic Faith, a Trinitarian-Fundamental Evangelistic Organization: Its Origin, Functions, Doctrinal Heritage, and Departmental Activities of Evangelism*. Portland, Ore.: Apostolic Faith Publishing House, 1965.

Bartleman, Frank. *How Pentecost Came to Los Angeles*. Los Angeles, Calif.: F. Bartleman, 1925.

Bills, V. Alex. "The Houston Connection: After Topeka and before Azusa Street." Paper delivered to the 30th Annual Meeting of the Society for Pentecostal Studies. Kirkland, Washington, March 16–18, 2000.

Buck, G. J. *The Free Christian: What and Where is the Christian Religion?* Waco, Tex.: Hill, Kellner, Frost, 1906.

Burgess, Stanley M., Gary Magee, and Patrick H. Alexander. *Dictionary of Pentecostal and Charismatic Movements.* Grand Rapids, Mich.: Zondervan Publishing House, 1988.

Burgess, Stanley M. and Eduard van der Mass. *The New Dictionary of Pentecostal and Charismatic Movements.* Grand Rapids, Mich: Zondervan Publishing House, 2002.

Clemmons, Ithiel. *Bishop C. H. Mason and the Roots of the Church of God in Christ.* Bakersfield, Calif.: Pneuma Life Publications, 1996.

Conn, Charles. *Where the Saints Have Trod: A History of Church of God Missions.* Cleveland, Tenn.: Pathway Press, 1959.

Corum, Fred T. *Like as of Fire: Newspapers from the Azusa Street World Wide Revival.* Washington, D.C.: Mid Atlantic Regional Press, 1988.

Corum, Fred T., and Hazel Blackwell. *The Sparkling Fountain.* Windsor, Ohio: Corum and Associates, 1983.

Corum, Hazel E. "Early Days of Pentecostalism in Springfield, Missouri." Unpublished manuscript, n.d.

Corum, Lillie E. "History of the Pentecostal Church in Springfield, Missouri." Unpublished manuscript. 1925.

Crawford, Raymond. *The Light of Life Brought Healing: A Brief Sketch of the Life and Labors of Florence L. (Mother) Crawford 1872–1936.* Portland, Ore.: The Apostolic Faith Publishing House, 1955.

Crawford, Robert. *Sermons and Scriptural Studies.* Portland, Ore.: The Apostolic Faith Publishing House, 1965.

Crews, Mickey. *The Church of God: A Social History.* Knoxville, Tenn.: University of Tennessee Press, 1990.

Ewart, Frank J. *The Phenomenon of Pentecost*. Hazelwood, Mo.: Word Aflame Press, 1975.

Faupel, William. *The Everlasting Gospel: The Significance of Eschatology in the Development of Pentecostal Thought*. Sheffield, England: Sheffield Academic Press, 1996.

Frodsham, Stanley. *With Signs Following: The Story of the Pentecostal Revival in the Twentieth Century*. Springfield, Mo.: Gospel Publishing House, 1946.

Goff, Jeff. *Fields White unto Harvest: Charles F. Parham and the Missionary Origins of Pentecostalism*. Fayetteville: University of Arkansas Press, 1988.

Goss, Ethel. *The Winds of God*. New York: Comet Press Books, 1958.

Harvey, Paul. *Freedom's Coming: Religion, Race, And Culture In The South, 1860–2000*. Los Angeles, Calif.: University of California Press, 2005.

Longman, Jr., Robert. "Pre-Pentecostalist History." Spirithome.com: Resource for Spirituality and Faith. http://www.spirithome.com/histpent.html.

Lum, Clara. Clara Lum to T. B. Barratt. University of Oslo Archives, T.B. Barratt Etterlatte Papirer, MS 4? 33412, Daghalter. IX, 53, cited in David Bundy, "Spiritual Advice to a Seeker: Letters to T. B. Barratt from Azusa Street, 1906." *Pneuma* 14 (Fall 1992): 159–70.

Martin, Larry, ed. *The Doctrines and Discipline of the Azusa Street Apostolic Faith Mission of Los Angeles*. Vol. 7. *The Complete Azusa Street Library*. Joplin, Mo.: Christian Life Books, 2000.

———. *The Life and Ministry of William J. Seymour*. Vol. 1. *The Complete Azusa Street Library*. Joplin, Mo.: Christian

Life Books, 1999.

———. *The Topeka Outpouring of 1901.* Joplin, Mo.: Christian Life Books, 2000.

———. *True Believers.* Vol. 2. *The Complete Azusa Street Library.* Joplin, Mo.: Christian Life Books, 1999.

———. *True Believers II.* Vol. 3. *The Complete Azusa Street Library.* Joplin, Mo.: Christian Life Books, 1999.

Mitchell, Robert E. *Heritage and Horizons: The History of the Open Bible Standard Churches.* Des Moines, Iowa: Open Bible Standard Churches, 1982.

Nelson, J. Douglas. "For Such a Time as This: The Story of Bishop William J. Seymour and the Azusa Street Revival, a Search for Pentecostal/Charismatic Roots." Ph.D. diss., University of Birmingham, England, 1981.

Nichols, John. *Pentecostalism.* Plainfield, N.J.: Logos International, 1966.

Nickel, Thomas R. *Azusa Street Outpouring: As Told to Me by Those Who Were There.* Hanford, Calif.: Great Commission International, 1979.

Owens, Robert. *Speak to the Rock—The Azusa Street Revival: Its Roots and Its Message.* Lanham, Md.: University Press of America, 2001.

Parham, Sarah E. *The Life of Charles F. Parham, Founder of the Apostolic Faith Movement.* New York: Garland Pub., 1985.

Sanchez-Walsh, Arlene. *Latino Pentecostal Identity: Evangelical Faith, Self, and Society.* New York: Columbia University Press, 2003.

Seymour, William J. 1999. *Words that Changed the World.* Vol. 5. *The Complete Azusa Street Library.* Joplin, Mo.: Christian Life Books, 1999.

Shumway, Charles. "A Critical History of Glossolalia." Ph.D. diss., Boston University, 1919.

————. A Study of the Gift of Tongues. N.p., 1914.

Sizelove, Rachel. "A Sketch of My Life." Unpublished manuscript, 1925.

————. "A Sparkling Fountain for the Whole Earth." *Word and Work* 56, no. 6 (June 1934).

Taylor, William. *The Flaming Torch in Darkest Africa.* New York: Eaton & Mains, 1898.

Thompson, Steve, and Adam Gordon. *A 20th Century Apostle: The Life of Alfred Garr.* Charlotte, N.C.: Morning Star Publications, 2003.

Tyson, James. *The Early Pentecostal Revival: History of the Twentieth Century Pentecostals and the Pentecostal Assemblies of the World, 1901–1930.* Hazelwood, Mo.: World Aflame, 1992.

Wacker, Grant. *Heaven Below. Early Pentecostals and American Culture.* Cambridge, Mass.: Harvard University Press, 2001.

Woodworth-Etta, Maria. *A Diary of Signs and Wonders.* Tulsa, Okla.: Harrison House, 1919.

Valdez, Alfred C., Jr. *Divine Health.* Chattanooga, Tenn. N.p., n.d.

————. *Fire on Azusa Street.* Costa Mesa, Calif.: Gift Publications, 1980.

Vanzandt, J.C. *Speaking in Tongues: A Discussion of Speaking in Tongues, Pentecost, Latter Rain, Evidence of the Holy Spirit Baptism and a Short History of the Tongues Movement in America and Some Foreign Countries.* Portland, Ore.: Vanzandt Publications, 1926.

Titled Articles

Alvarez, Carmelo E. "Hispanic Pentecostals: Azusa Street and Beyond." *Cyberjournal for Pentecostal-Charismatic Research* 5 (February 1999).

"A Message from Mr. & Mrs. Mead." *Confidence* (15 November 1908): 18.

"Azusa's First Camp-Meeting." *Word and Work* 58, no. 1 (1936): 1.

Betancourt, Esdras. "Hispanic Pentecostals: History and Mission." Paper delivered to the 23rd Annual Meeting of the Society for Pentecostal Studies, 11–13 November 1993, Guadalajara, Mexico.

Blumhofer, Edith M., and Grant Wacker. "Who Edited the Azusa Street Mission's Apostolic Faith?" *Assemblies of God Heritage* 21 (Summer 2001): 20.

Boddy, Alexander A. "Some Los Angeles Friends." *Confidence* (November 1912).

Burgess, Stanley. "Pentecostalism in India: An Overview." *Asian Journal of Pentecostal Studies* 4, no. 1 (2001): 85–98.

"Color Line Obliterated." *The Morning Oregonian* (Portland), 31 December 1906, 4.

"Converts Claim Strange Power." *The Evening Review* (East Liverpool, Ohio), 7 January 1907, 1, 3.

Corum, J. J. "A Sparking Fountain for the Whole Earth," *Word and Work* 56 (July 1934): 7.

Cotton, Emma. "The Inside Story of the Outpouring of the Holy Spirit—Azusa Street—April 1906." *Message of the Apostolic Faith* 1:1 (April 1936).

Espinosa, Gaston. "Tongues and Healing at the Azusa Street Revival." Vol. 2, *Religions of the United States in Practice.* Edited by Colleen McDannell. Princeton, N.J.: Princeton University Press, 2001. 217–23.

———. "The Silent Pentacostals." *Christian History Issue* 58, 17, no. 2 (1998): 23–24.

Garr, Mrs. A. G. "Pentecostal Power." *The Latter Rain* (March 1907): 1–2.

Hanna, Ghalia. "Egypt: Apostolic Faith Mission House." *Confidence* (1 January 1909): 22.

"Healed Blind Woman. 'Tonguers' Also Claimed to Have Cured Mr. Smith of a Cancer." *Daily Capital Journal* (Salem, Ore.), 24 December 1906.

"How Pentecost Came to Ohio in 1906." *Assembly of God Heritage* (1988): 4.

"How Pentecost Reached Ohio in Dec. 1906." *Assembly of God Heritage* 8, no. 1 (Spring 1988): 4.

Hyatt, Susan. "Spirit Filled Women." In *The Century of the Holy Spirit: 100 Years of Pentecostal and Charismatic Renewal.* Edited by Vinson Synan. Nashville, Tenn.: Thomas Nelson Publishers, 2001. 233–63.

Ketcham, Maynard, and Wayne Warner. "When the Pentecostal Fire Fell in Calcutta: A/G Missions Traces Origin To 1907 Outpourings." *Assemblies of God Heritage* 3, no. 3 (Fall 1983): 5–6.

Lee, B. C. "When God Breathed on Zion." In *Out of Zion: Into All the World.* Edited by Gordon P. Gardiner. Shippensburg, Pa.: Companion Press, 1990.

Leatherman, Lucy. "A Missionary Trip through Syria and Palestine." *The Pentecost* (1 December 1908): 5.

———. "Apostolic Revival in Egypt." *The Pentecost* (January–February 1909): 5.

———. "Brief notes: The Philippines." *Confidence* (15 February 1910): 15.

———. "Coming Home." *The Pentecost* (15 September 1909): 4.

———. "Jerusalem." *Confidence* (15 March 1912): 11.

———. "Letter from Sister Lucy." *The Pentecost* (1 December 1908): 5.

———. "Syria: News." *Confidence* (15 August 1912): 17.

———. "Your Good Letter." *The Pentecost* (1 July 1908): 6.

"Manifestations Continue, Many Different Experiences. The Los Angeles Mission Reports to Miss Clara E. Lum," *Missionary World* (August 1906): 8.

"Meeting Closes Early. Unknown Tongues Mute, Unknown Script Paralized Last Night." *Daily Capital Journal* (Salem, Ore.), 28 December 1906.

"News from Miss Lucy Leatherman." *Confidence* (August 1912): 185.

Olsen, Ted. "American Pentecost: The Story Behind the Azusa Street Revival, the Most Phenomenal Event of Twentieth Century Christianity." *Christian History*. Issue 58, vol. 17, no. 2 (1998): 14.

Robeck, Cecil M., Jr. "Florence Crawford: Apostolic Faith Pioneer." In *Portraits of a Generation: Early Pentecostal Leaders*. Edited by Grant Wacker and James R. Goff, Jr. Little Rock: University of Arkansas Press, 2002.

Sizelove, Rachel. "The Temple." *Word and Work* 58 (May 1936): 1.

"Slow To Arrive: Tongues of Fire Evangelists from Los Angeles Not Here—Expected Daily." *Daily Oregon Statesman,* 10 October 1906, 2.

"The Gift of Tongues is Satan's Work." *Los Angeles Record.*

Tinney, James. "William J. Seymour: Father of Modern-Day Pentecostalism." In Randall Burkett and Richard Newmans, eds., *Black Apostles: Afro-American Clergy Confront the Twentieth Century.* Boston: G. K. Hall, 1978. 213–25.

"Tongues Gift is Denounced." *Los Angeles Times,* 1907.

"Under Wings of Police." *Daily Capital Journal* (Salem, Ore.), 14 November 1906.

Tuthill, H. G. "History of the Latter Rain." *The Faithful Standard* (July 1922).

Valdez, A. C. "From Catholicism to Pentecost: Saved and Called to God's Service." *Latter Rain Evangel* (February 1923): 15–19.

"Victory to the Soul Who Brooks No Denial: How Wrestling with God Transformed Lives," *Latter Rain Evangel* (January 1923): 2–5, 13–14.

Walling, Aaron. "An Evaluation of the Apostolic Faith: The 1906–08 Revival Paper." *Assemblies of God Heritage* 19 (Summer 1999): 10–15.

Titled Articles from *The Apostolic Faith*

"Ask What You Will," 1, no. 2 (October 1906): 3.

"Bible Pentecost," 1, no. 3 (November 1906): 1.

Bowen, Pearl. "Akron Visited by Pentecost," 1, no. 5 (January 1907): 1.

"Bro. G. W. Batman's Testimony," 1, no. 4 (December 1906): 4.

"Brother Mead's Testimony of Pentecost," 1, no. 3 (November 1906): 3.

"Brother Ryan Receives His Pentecost," 1, no. 3 (November 1906): 3.

Campbell, Ivy. "Report from Ohio and Pennsylvania," 1, no. 6 (February–March 1907): 4.

"Demons Cast Out," 1, no. 6 (February 1907): 3.

"Enroute to Africa," 1, no. 4 (December 1906): 4.

Farrow, Lucy. "The Work in Virginia," 1, no. 2 (October 1906): 3.

"Fire Falling in Oakland," 1, no. 1 (September 1906): 4.

"A Girl's Consecration for Africa," 1, no. 2 (October 1906): 1.

"Gracious Pentecostal Showers Continue to Fall," 1, no. 3 (November 1906): 1.

Hall, Anna. "Honor the Holy Ghost," 1, no. 2 (October 1906): 4.

———. "The Polishing Process," 1, no. 2 (October 1906): 4.

———. "Jesus is Coming," 1, no. 1 (September 1906): 4.

"In Africa," 1, no. 7 (April 1907): 1.

"Jerusalem," 1, no. 13 (May 1908): 1.

"Latest Report from our Missionaries to Africa," 1, no. 5 (January 1907): 3.

Lum, Clara. "Pentecostal Testimonies," 1, no. 6 (February 1907): 4.

"A Message Concerning His Coming," 1, no. 2 (October 1906): 3.

"Missionaries' Farewell," 1, no. 2 (October 1906): 4.

"Missionaries to Jerusalem," 1, no.1 (September 1906): 4.

Moore, Jennie Evans. "Music from Heaven," 1, no. 8 (May 1907): 3.

"Mrs. Daisy Batman's Testimony," 1, no. 4 (December 1906): 4.

"New-Tongued Missionaries," 1, no. 3 (November 1906): 2.

Ophelia Wiley. "Sermon on a Dress," 1, no. 2 (October 1906): 2.

"Pentecost in Danville," 1, no. 2 (October 1906): 2.

"Pentecost in Middle States," 1, no. 6 (February 1907): 3.

"Pentecost in New York," 1, no. 4 (December 1906): 4.

"Pentecost in Woodland," 1, no. 4 (December 1906): 1.

"Pentecostal Experience," 1, no. 3 (November 1906): 4.

"Pentecostal Meetings," 1, no. 8 (May 1907): 1.

"Preaching to the Spanish," 1, no. 3 (November 1906): 4.

"Received Her Pentecost," 1, no. 5 (January 1907): 3.

"Report from Ohio and Pennsylvania," 1, no. 6 (February–March 1907): 5.

"Russians Hear in their Own Tongue," 1, no. 1 (September 1906): 4.

"The Same Old Way," 1, no. 1 (September 1906): 1.

"San Francisco and Oakland," 1, no. 4 (December 1906): 4.

Seymour, William Joseph. "Bible Teaching on Marriage and Divorce," 1, no. 5 (January 1907): 3.

———. "The Marriage Tie," 1, no. 10 (September 1907): 3.

"Sister Hutchins' Testimony," 1, no. 2 (October 1906): 1.

"Sister Mead's Baptism," 1, no. 3 (November 1906): 3.

"Spanish Receive Pentecost," 1, no. 2 (October 1906): 4.

"Spreading the Gospel," 1, no. 3 (November 1906) 1.

Index